WHERE ARE THE HALOS?

BY RAY PIÑA

Where are the Halos?

Copyright © Ray Piña

TAOIST KNIGHT Publishing, LLC
TaoistKnightPublishing.com

For my mother. Who taught me to be anything I
wanted to be as long as I gave it my all.

And to The Mysterious God. Who fills me with
inspiration, wonder and insight.

CONTENTS

PREFACE
THE WAY IT IS

"A man may be born a slave in a pagan society or a feudal lord or a proletarian. What does not vary is the necessity for him to exist in the world, to be at work there, to be there in the midst of other people and to be mortal there."
— Jean-Paul Sartre

When my father was 5 years old my Abuelo took him to the outskirts of the fledgling farm in Camaguey, Cuba, and told him, "Son, when you are born with a pair of balls life is going to be hard; you better bust your ass."

Right after that, my father, at that tender age — probably tan and peeling, wondering what the hell he's doing in Cuba ... with a dirt floor ... with a cow for milk ... with a rifle to shoot shit — commenced to build a wooden fence. And he continued to build that fence morning, noon and night for months until it was done.

Me? I was spared. I didn't get hit with that shit 'till I was 7.

I remember being passenger-side in my dad's proud Buick Regal. He busted his ass for it, but it was luxurious ... good bass; polished-wooden dashboard. We'd tap to the music on it at red lights or in the garage after he picked me up from Karate ... sometimes he'd let me drive it in. I remember him looking at me. He was still young with a head full of black tight curly hair … younger than I am now. *Scary!* His burden! Three kids and the weight of the world!

He was doing it though. He was pulling it off. And he did it quietly like a man.

Never a complaint!

A chin-never-down, keep-your-head-up-and-take-on-the-world motherfucker.

Potentially mean, but also overly sensitive with a naïve child's soul … mean only out of necessity to face the world he had seen, the hardened experiences he had been through.

He turned forward, hung his arm out the Buick window and that was it — too cool for his own good. He said what he had to say … the whole thing about the balls, the hard-knock life.

I remember seeing some homeless guys shuffling around on the side of McCarter Highway. They didn't have bottles in paper bags. Not like on TV … they were too far gone for that. They were nearly apparitions.

Those guys didn't look like they were working too hard, certainly not *busting their ass.*

"What about them?" I asked.

"Those," my dad said. "They're bums."

Part I:

Ignorant Without Bliss

Chapter 1:

UPS Underground

"Prepare a place to slaughter his sons for the sins of their forefathers; they are not to rise to inherit the land and cover the earth with their cities." – Isaiah 14:21

I guess I got lucky. It was like I did forty fast spins, stopped and there I was sitting in the Human Resources department of UPS with all the other bums … restless. Wanting the job; but wanting the hell out of that place at the same time … as soon as possible! Beat … and we ain't even begun.

Pathetic … every one of them … half dead already … pimply … yellowed by drug and booze you name it. It didn't look like they could get it together to cross moderate traffic, never mind carry heavy boxes. Ageless: 30 or 55 who would know?

Me? I'm decked out in my Catholic Schoolboy outfit; hair held in place with something or other. I checked the mirror before leaving.

Did I have a job before?

"No."

How do I know I could handle the work? It's not easy. Most guys quit after a few days; a week tops.

"My father's Cuban and was a longshoreman at Port Newark; he raised me to bust my ass."

That was it. He shook my hand looking lucky to be on the other side of the desk. His pants were short, and I could see his hairy legs … a real cheap suit. Something you'd pick up in a Secaucus outlet. A white and black striped shirt with a thin leather tie … the shirt was visibly stained. Not blotched, but it had taken on a yellow hue.

There was no second interview. Just an after-dinner phone call and an order to be at such-and-such location by 5 … *You might want to bring a work belt.*

"a.m. or p.m.?"

p.m.!

That was it.

And what a location! Splendid! The heart of downtown Newark! So downtown actually East Orange … pure ghetto!

I search out the district manager and shake his hand. He's about 40, tall, thinning mid-length hair … how did he get in charge? Turns out he's a surfer and a racist. I'm half up his alley already. He's talking to me like I'm not a spic. It's hard to tell.

He introduces me to line manager Mike who's 25. He's sporting jeans; a white short-sleeved, buttoned-down shirt; and that same thin black-leather tie … maybe he shops with the guy from human resources? But that's another world safely tucked away in Secaucus. Nobody here but us dogs; I sense it already.

Mike shows me where to punch in and lets me even though it's only 4:40 p.m. My dad always told me to be early. Not on time: Early.

Pointing down an elevated aluminum alley, like some gallows, manager Mike shows me my new home and informs me that I'll be on *his* crew.

I do what I have to do while killing some company time … I take a shit … Good enough! … I was expecting worse from a shit hole like that … clean and spacious with toilet paper to spare. "OK," I said to myself. "I can work here."

The environment itself is doable but bleak. Everywhere you look just boxes going down conveyer belts. Boxes shimmying up and out of trucks; laborers noticeably in a trance picking them off — on the brink of being overwhelmed by boxes but not quite yet … the whole thing will soon shut down for the shift change.

Boxes carried along gigantic shoots, hopping from conveyer belt to conveyer belt — often double decked: two tiers … horizontal rivers flowing boxes. Little brown trucks scooting them away … that's where the money's supposed to be. Those guys are the hierarchy. The knights.

At five o'clock the buzzer lets out an ungodly roar, more of a death howl: eeeeaaaarrrrrrrrrrrrrrrrrrrrnnnnnnnnnnnnnn!!!!

I'm engulfed by an 18-wheeler realizing these things look a lot bigger from the inside — empty and alone — than passing them on the N.J. Turnpike at 75 m.p.h. … it's just me and a line of shoulder-high rollers running down the container's center … it's not encouraging.

The boxes start coming. It's not too tough at first; I can handle the pace. Pulling the boxes down off the roller isn't too bad, either; their weight does most of the work. I just have to control their descent, stack them tight-like against the container's front wall — roller high — and work my way towards the back … I can work like this for hours, no problem.

And the money's good: $8 an hour; $10.50 if I can make it through the month … The Union! They tell me it's all about The Union. Local some-thing-or-other.

The trouble starts about 40 minutes into the shift when you realize you milked the lower level for all it's worth. There's simply no more room. Only one thing left to do: lower the flaps ... the first time I did the fucker closed right on my head. The latch wasn't secured properly. It was missing a couple screws … I could've walked right out of that place with a lawsuit Day 1 … no training, faulty rig. Instead, I closed the other flaps and hopped on top to find the truck looking empty once again, only now the rollers were at my toes and I had to stack to the roof. The boxes automatically seem bigger, heavier.

No time for doubt! Dig in! It's waaaaaay too early to be thinking about that … and you know what that is … "hasta luego!"

Can't do it! Not even an option; not this early in the game … I've yet to prove my mettle to myself, let alone my old man.

So, I tighten my lifting belt. What else can ya do? My dad got it for me when I joined the powerlifting team in high school. It was nice; real leather … I had no job at the time. "Varsity Athlete." I was milking the title.

Here they come! Marching! … boxes with smirks on their faces … bending — hands to toes —— to pick them up. Heavy boxes! All sizes! In some crazy scheme the little ones weigh more than the big ones! Incredible! Unbelievable! An eight-inch package: 45 pounds! And at your toes! … wobbling along the roller and no wonder it had all these other boxes piled up behind it … a logjam on the great river UPS. And I thought I was going to one hand the fucker ... Bullshit! It wasn't even a box! A bundle of brown packing tape … non-specific in shape but very heavy and dense. Gold? Lead? Who's sending this shit?

You can't stack those fuckers properly either. Picking this thing off the roller I ponder my pathetic wall of boxes. Where is it going to go?

On the left, not too bad: straight and stacked tight. It wasn't really me; it was the boxes. Big, well-defined boxes but light ... like Christmas presents. It gave my wall a sense of structure: about 8 feet tall with a little wiggle room at the top.

The middle? Oh God; the middle was pathetic. Real bad. Caving in already and only chest high, like a crumbling wave. This thing wasn't going to last! He gave me a pep talk about it, the line manager ... the guy with the thin leather tie. "Do your best," he said. "Just make it tight. Ya got to make it tight."

Tight ... OK, I got it.

This thing was less than tight. This wall was Loose Lucy ... its tendency was towards chaos, collapse.

"Fuck it!" I said to myself. "This thing's going right here." I balance the demon package atop my cresting wave ... something tells me I shouldn't have built so high on the left so soon. Later, I learned not to look at them as single boxes but to create geometric clumps with several boxes. Still, taped barbells just weren't my thing.

To make matters worse, Gator, our crew's picker, was absent ... he didn't call out either. He decided to surprise everybody.

Poor manager Mike was having a hell of a time; would've had his sleeves rolled up if he had a pair... he'd better watch that tie, though. Getting choked out by the conveyer belt while unclogging boxes isn't as romantic as it sounds.

Surfer Joe, the KKK district manager, he came over and really gave it to Mikey.

Even locked in my tin can I knew the score: we were backing up the whole joint! Our mess was affecting all the other lines.

"It's usually not this bad. Just do the best ya can."

I appreciated Mike's comforting remarks, but I wasn't sure if they were fueled by kindness or a fear that I'd just jet and he'd be left alone with Manny, the Portuguese kid who was packed in the sardine can next door doing all he could to manage his own flash flood of boxes.

Manny was generally liked by everyone; not an easy feat for a White Kid … well, White-ish. It helped that he was Portuguese. But just because the Blacks will tolerate you doesn't mean they'll respect you. And even if they respect you — especially if they respect you — you're open for chastisement. As for Mikey, make no bones about it: no one could stand his Irish/Italian ass … especially the Surf Nazi! He despised that Mikey was appointed manager by a leveraged relative and not through tenure humping boxes like the rest of us.

Fuck doing the best I could, I was surviving.

The brief logjam gave me an opportunity to catch up, but only momentarily. As soon as I cleared things away enough to sneak a few peeks, see what's going on under the warehouse's halogen lights, Mikey pulls me out and past Manny's truck … I didn't get a glimpse at his wall of boxes … he was in too deep and dark. They don't waste a lightbulb on us. But I was curious as all hell.

Now I'm in another truck. This oddball isn't a full jobber; it's about 2/3rds the size of the behemoth they pulled me out of and there's no lower chamber. You step in on the ground floor and get to loading. You start thinking, "Why didn't they pull Manny out of his truck?" Maybe they figured my walls needed work. There certainly were plenty of boxes to practice with. Maybe Manny was just smart. Maybe Manny learned the boxes are going to keep coming so you might as well pace yourself. Either way, there are boxes everywhere and you better be careful. Even the ones that don't have some odd loose pointy thing sticking out of them somewhere — usually on their blind side — even those can get ya … No shit? Like I didn't figure that out by 5:01 p.m.

I straighten everything up; that's the best I can do at this point. I feel like I can get away with it: it's my first day; *"it's never this bad;"* I didn't sign on to this truck; blah, blah, blah … Where's Gator?

They send me back to my original truck. Shit is pretty bad again. To spare himself, Necktie-Mikey cleared the jam by double- and triple stacking the boxes onto my roller. Now it wasn't just the entire length of the truck, but the entire length x 3 … with spills everywhere!

The horrifying buzzer sounds again and I don't know what it means. Is there more coming? Are we doubling up? What we just did x 2? … 'cause I can't handle it.

"Break, Ray."

That's all Manny said passing my truck, stepping over the few boxes littering the alley of our gang's wing … three trucks docked and loading.

⸻ ∽∽ ⸻

Boxes! Disgusted by boxes! Boxes for kicking, boxes for punching, for stomping to fit in any ol' way just to get 'em out of my face … boxes.

Where do you want them?

Stacked tight?

Well, how about that three-foot opening I left at the top of my pathetic wall? How 'bout I just start throwing some of this shit right through there? I know there's nothing worth a damn holding it up … let the whole thing collapse for all I care! Just drag me out when the boxes settle … Don't mind me sir, just doing the best I can … it's usually not this bad, right?

Up and over! I can hear shit falling behind this phony baloney wall I've concocted. Anytime manager Mike wasn't looking: packages up and over, up and over.

10

I better start making it look good though, my cave was getting exposed; it was filling up. I was working near the rear. What a pathetic wall: twice as weak as it looked … don't lean on it!

I gave up on the water bottle. Did I mention there was no time for a piss, let alone stop and have a swig as I watch the tide come in … big full-moon weather advisory of boxes. Baton down the hatches! Wear your booties bro, you're gonna need 'em.

Now what the fuck is this?

At first my eyes don't believe it; couldn't comprehend it. Like the game of Tetris had just been turned up a notch … who's playing with the controls? That's not square! That's not even a heavy-as-fuck pile of brown tape … that shit's cylindrical, a bucket!

"What do I do with this," I asked, as if shoving it any old place could further compromise the integrity of my wiggly wall. As soon as this coach is hitched and the guy pulls out: tons of boxes lunging to the rear … no doubt about that. A guarantee.

Don't worry about 'em, he says. *Just stack 'em to the side*, he says. All right with me. At least the buckets have a handle, makes it easier to pick 'em off the roller… or so you'd think.

And then, just like that — out of nowhere — he tells me I can go … a cheerfulness like you couldn't imagine! A new life! … one without boxes.

I hopped out of the container and noticed the place had quieted down. All the other lines were packed up for the night — loading zone doors down, trucks long gone and on the road.

"What time is it?"

Ten minutes to 10:00 … Turns out he *was* pretty cool, letting me bounce ten minutes early and all. It was probably best that I wasn't around when he got a good sight of that wall, anyway. What a disaster.

Outside (I skedaddled before anyone changed their mind), the summer night was crisp and clear. There would've been stars if it wasn't Newark but it was quiet just the same.   No, the locals stayed the hell away for the most part. They wanted nothing to do with that place … I didn't blame them.

———

So, let me tell you about Gator … and the loafing … and the showing up 10- to 15 minutes late … and cutting out 10- to 15 minutes early … for this … for that … for any ol' damn reason … because he feels like it! Because his boys are calling for him from out under the cargo-bay doors … to drink a 40oz. … to smoke a blunt. At the same time he was the best damn picker in the place — everybody knew it, even the neckties. That's how he got away with his shit.

Thirty-something, black and obnoxious, he loved busting my balls.

"Hey, white boy. It's still early … you going to make it?"

Me? I'd give it right back to him. "I don't know Gator; these boxes are feeling kind of heavy. We might get backed up tonight."

Nobody wanted that. They'd make it look like it's his fault. They'd make it look like it's my fault. But in reality, you can only handle so many boxes per minute. When the levee breaks, there really ain't nowhere to go but under.

Gator knew his business though, and, if anything he took his time, set a nice pace — it wasn't too bad. He had a knack for it. A few times when he was out, they tried having me pick. It was nice standing outside the truck and all, but I couldn't read the zip codes fast enough. A lot of the boxes were getting by me. They'd go around the entire works again. Around where the brown trucks were unloading. Past the general sorters, a group of five or six guys scooting boxes down various shoots and off to individual lines. Yeah, a lot got past me. It held everybody up. It didn't take them long to figure out I was best off in the truck like an animal. After a while it became a mantra: "Boxes! Give me boxes!"

I received a few negative reports from Philly, our line's receiving port: *Your walls are shit!*

Really? Get out of here; you have to be kidding me. You don't see the Picasso-esque nature of these walls? … Cubism! … Cubism! Every man has his style, no?

No! Make 'em tighter!

It was like that a lot, too. It wasn't all peachy. Not so much from Gator — Gator was cool; Gator wanted to chill and just make it through the shift — but from the neckties; both of them.

We expected it from Surf Nazi … balding fuck. He wasn't bald yet, but I saw it … his cue-ball destiny. And boy was he mad about it … But the young kid, our line manager Mikey, he could be a real prick. Start cursing and yelling —— *screaming!* — on the drop of a dime, and then try to be all cool, hunky-dory about it five minutes later.

Yeah, right! Go fuck yourself! Getting all bent out of shape over a backed-up line. What the fuck ya want us to do? We're *stacking* as fast as we can. And "stacking" just to throw the hardest job in the place right back in his face. Not picking! Not driving little brown trucks or making sales! And certainly not standing around all cushy who-do-I-know managing. Get the fuck out of my face.

Of course, I didn't say it … hell no! By that time they got ya by the balls. Soon as you accept the fucking job: All excited. Come home and tell your gal: "I got the job." Hurray. Hurray. Your dreams have come true … actually on your knees praying for it, picturing how it will save every sorrow. More cash! Ooh, maybe a new car … you start thinking about pussy, stepping it up a notch. Can almost smell it on your hand already. Isn't it great?

Look! The pussy gets thrown up in the air … some of its going to fall on ya eventually. Slap yourself! Wake up Jack! Who you slaving away for anyway?

My mother had just died but I had Tracey. I was young. I was young. That's what was going through my mind. I'll get into a school eventually. I was going to be a millionaire stockbroker by 30 … big house on Long Island … maybe write a book about it. Yeah, the things ya tell yourself to pass the time. It's in the doing buddy. And you're buried in boxes.

CHAPTER 2:

A SHORT REPRIEVE

"It's true. Hard work never killed anybody; but I figure, why take the chance?" – Ronald Reagan, actor/U.S. president

I got a pardon. I appealed to my higher self and why the fuck not?

It didn't escape me that everyone was sneaking off to school … and they weren't exactly packing my picture.

Rob Wondolowski got a full ride … he could barely read! His folks got him "Hooked on Phonics" in 9th Grade.

Tracey? She was going to teach!

Teach!

She argued with me that it was impossible to drive to Alaska.

I told her I did in 6th Grade. I insisted … Yellowstone, British Columbia, Valdez, the Arctic Circle … whole family round trip in a van. I showed her the photo album.

"Impossible," she said, "It's *all the way down there, an island,*" as she pointed to the boxed-off state tucked away in the lower-left-hand corner of the map.

Now, I'll give somebody the benefit of the doubt. Canada and Mexico were not represented … a purely jingo map! … and the perspective … with Alaska and Hawaii side-by-side hiding out in the corner … a little off … no doubt about it. But the snow, Tracey! The snow! Can't you recall the Eskimos? The igloos? The dog sleds? There weren't any grass skirts and coconut bras, were there?

It wasn't like I impressed anyone with my S.A.T. … so low I didn't bother to remember the score. And the coaches weren't exactly fond of my ass senior year, that's for sure. I lost interest. Junior year was the year… Undefeated! That was the team! But senior year: 8 and 2 … a total disgrace. No State Championship! No First Team All-State honors! … not for being with those bums.

Rob was the star player, so he got star player treatment: interviews after the game, pictures in the paper diving into the end zone … not fifth- or sixth paragraph mentions like some people we know.

"Hey, coach. How about me? I'm captain, too. There's three of us, ya know." The other co-captain … Jason Gilbert, our quarterback … amazing athlete! Varsity letter holder since sophomore year like someone you know… get your fingers ready to count … baseball, basketball, football. He'd hold onto the ball and book his skinny ass 'round the corner … it was usually good for 15- or 20 yards; it wasn't unusual for him to break one all the way.

Maybe the papers didn't want to hear from Jason and me, but the coaches weren't rushing to place the mic under our noses either … we had shit to say. We were there. If you look close enough — beyond the guy with the football — you'd see me in the photo, too. I'm the guy twisted up in a pile of bodies, Rob literally running over my back to glory … maybe someone else could have made the same block … after a summer of Double Sessions, after hitting the Seven-Man Sled all season after class … but it was me there.

I was distracted senior year, though. I'll give the coaches that.

Those early summer camps, the practices we weren't supposed to be having — at least according to the intramural rules…. they didn't appeal to me. Not as much as sneaking down the shore with my mom and brother to go surfing.

We were learning … about more than the surf.

Apparently, my dad was not keen on my mother joining the work-force … there was aggression. Tension. Everyone's stomach in a knot … my mother accused him of infidelity; waved a lipstick-stained white shirt over the second-floor banister. Like a war flag. Not of defeat, but of liberation.

I didn't yet know about his coke problem. And my mom didn't know that the pain in her shoulder — the one our ancient Polish sha-man was treating with Cortisone shots — was lymphoma. It wouldn't take long. She lasted the season. By Christmas she was hooked up to a breathing machine in the living room … don't trip over the tubes or wires!

She died graduation morning.

Regardless, the coaches weren't bragging about me. I'd like to think it was racial, that it was a Cuban thing. But Jason Gilbert is as white as they come and they didn't let him say "boo" either.

Speaking of diversity, I started thinking I didn't belong in a sweat-box of a tin can loading boxes at UPS; that somehow, I deserved better.

I could handle the labor! Let's make that clear. But when you're surrounded by grown men with wives and kids and you see them struggling, wiping sweat and holding their backs and the biggest bur-den isn't the boxes … I had to start making some executive decisions.

Just about this time, Mark Blanco, God bless his soul, the biggest pot head I knew — the guy who failed miserably trying to squeeze his used Firebird between a row of parked cars and a lazy garbage truck — shared an epiphany with me: why don't I try to get on the football team at St. Peter's College?

Now, I never heard of St. Peter's College. And when he told me it was in Jersey City, well, the traditional cheerleader/keg-stand collegiate imagery faded fast ... I was thinking about locking up my mother's car; making sure The Club was firmly in place *and* very visible.

Mark got accepted. I think it had more to do with his baseball stats than academic credentials but that was exactly the kind of mentoring I needed ... he advised a highlight tape.

Luckily for me, not only did Comcast Cable air most of our games but my parents collected that sort of memorabilia ... two VCRs, a couple twisted joints, some fancy wiring and we were in business.

We skipped over the occasional missed block or tackle but made sure to include EVERY sack I ever had ... we went deep into the archive, all the way back to sophomore year. Of course, if they asked, we'd say it was to show my depth, how I performed at the varsity level even as a young lad. But between you and me, it's because there weren't that many sacks to go around ... maybe five or six good ones, where you can definitely see it's me and not a group effort.

I did have one thing going for me though: I sent that fucker UPS Next Day Air ... not Second- or Third-Day ... Next Day! And why the fuck not? The materials were there. Didn't matter if it was only crossing the Passaic River, skipping three miles from Newark to Jersey City ... *Attention: St. Peter's College Athletic Dept.!*

CHAPTER 3:

A REAL CHAMP

"Labor disgraces no man; unfortunately, you occasionally find men who disgrace labor." – Ulysses S. Grant

So, the football thing didn't work out. I know what ya want to hear: that they were too big; that I couldn't handle the jump from high school to college … I know your type.

But when I tell ya I handled my own even though I was the only one not jacked up on steroids, I really mean it was the pot. And when I tell ya I was running to Hawthorne Ave. every night with Mark for dime bags, I'm really saying it was the surf. And when I say it was the surf, I mean it was me … I just doggone changed.

It lasted a while; wasn't like I didn't try. I liked the way they did my laundry: Just hang the netted bag and there it was the next day … *woala!* right back in the locker … special delivery. Believe me, I took advantage; it wasn't all jerseys and jock straps.

The coaches loved me, too. They didn't know whether to line me up at tight end and get me the ball or keep me at outside linebacker

19

… I dumped the line captain, a 335 lbs. senior, right on his ass. All in all, I was a good fit. I had a place on the team.

But it quickly became evident that I couldn't go to battle with these guys.

You know the dickhead football players in high school? Well, these were the best of the best. The biggest dicks! A lot of them were criminals, too. But there was mostly this overwhelming sense of trying to hold on to something I didn't want to hold on to; especially with strangers. It was time to let go.

I wasn't exactly feeling the curfew, either. While I'm in bed black and blue Mark's picking up chicks at the school bar, going back to their dorms … fresh girls, girls from the Jersey shore who wanted to dorm close to Manhattan but with parents who insisted on Jersey City tuition and rent.

Then, one afternoon, Mark intercepts me on campus: "The surf's four- to six feet and offshore."

That's all he really had to say. I had my fill of football. I didn't need the pigskin to score.

Here's one you've heard: "It's not what ya know, it's who you know."

Well, my luck was about to change … *the opportunity of a lifetime* and what not. And whoa did I need it. For someone with no job and who was snorting a ton of coke, boy was my old man on my case: Get a job here … Get a job there … Get a job everywhere. If he had his way, I'd be working full time at The Port … *while going to school!*

Anyway, my ship had come in. My uncle — my mother's sister's husband — was hooking me up; he had something for me.

Ready?

… stock boy at CHAMPS!

Yeah, not too glamorous; I can admit it. Still with the fucking boxes ... only this time: unloading!

In actuality, it was a covert operation, an undercover assignment ... real hush hush. Of course, I still had to unload everything; that goes without saying. But there was a thief! Someone was making themself privy to the merchandise ... there was no stopping them. Every method must have been employed: checking people's bags as they punched out; cameras; bonus checks for months with no thievery ... surely, they tried it all. Because when I arrived none of this was in place. Just tons of merchandise everywhere ... *free* merchandise.

Dinner was provided; we had that luxury at home. Abuela the mistro ... pressure cookers, expresso pots, rice ... something going on every burner ... it was the background noise. Her little on-foot excursions to the grocery store ... frijoles negros, yucca, platanos, chicharron ... I was more than full.

St. Peter's Athletic Department didn't have shit on Abuela's laundry service.... Washed *and* ironed. My dress shirts were ready if I ever needed them.

The floors?

Mopped three times a week! Minimum! ... it was Escapades on Ice getting from the front door to the staircase.

Gave dad a full report when he made it home though, got to say it. The smoke! She couldn't take it ... coughing and complaining and knocking on my toweled bedroom door. "Ray Ray," in her broken English, "too much smoke. Me no breathe ... me no breathe ... too much." And then I'd hear her sigh and shuffle away and console myself thinking the language barrier excused my behavior.

I told him it was incense, which was partially true. He didn't believe me but never pushed the subject ... something about the frying pan calling the kettle black. Why argue? A freight train must've been storming through his brain. He looked wired and tired and wanting to vanish … he was working on it … day by day … it was his pet project.

Me? Oh, I was in heaven … Working! … Halle-fucking-lujah! Praise the lord! … another Piña on the job!

Once again: boxes by the bounty full … but pathetic … real pussy shit. The UPS guy did all the work. He was the one huffing it; unloading the fuckers in his drab brown uniform. Yeah, where are all the ladies now?

"The UPS guy!" "The UPS guy!"

Yeah, the UPS guy is breaking his back!

Me, the stock boy … Sitting pretty! Delicately cutting open boxes; creating semi-neat piles of inventory: socks, T-shirts, hockey sticks, baseball bats, soccer balls, you name it … sneakers were a pain-in-the-ass.

Six ceiling-high isles of sneakers in the back: Nike, Adidas, Reebok, Asics, New Balance, more … much more. Assorted by brand, style and size … Sell one … get three more in the next day. Got to shift the whole thing around again. Sometimes one brand would jump over into another's turf … it wasn't pretty.

On top of all this I was supposed to catch a thief. I took an unorthodox approach … I'd become the thief. I had my ways.

Rule No. 1: Don't get caught! Like jerking off, you better have a plan if someone walks in. Better yet … nobody walks in! … you find a way!

For example, I took T-shirts to the bathroom. I was the only one back there. Sure, every once in a while someone came back to grab something, a larger item … maybe a punching bag, a snowboard — this wasn't ghetto CHAMPS! This was Paramus Park Mall … damn would these ladies spend. A ton of crap for themselves! … tennis rackets, tank-tops, biker shorts … full-on, rich-bitch high maintenance … something for little Bobby … a skateboard, new basketball

... not the ball! The break-away-backboard with wheels. No birthday. No Christmas. Just because. Okay? You getting it?

Only now, alone in the bathroom, do I pull the T-shirt (still in its original wrapper) out from my waste band, from behind my back — a little presto change-o.

All in all, I'd have the new t-shirt on and covered by my original shirt in 15 seconds ... the entire task executed while on the crapper. Who's going to insist? Who's going to knock more than once, not let me be?

Rule No 2: Cover your tracks. Goes without saying, but you'd be surprised.

The T-shirt's plastic wrapper?

Gone! And not in the bathroom wastebasket! ... No, that shit went out in the trash with the legitimate discarded wrappers, with the boxes they arrived in ... the whole thing crunched in the huge mechanical garbage outback. And of course I checked the T-shirt off the manifest as if it came in, as if I folded it, placed it on the shelf or hung it out on the sales floor ... to any future inventory takers it would appear as if it had just disappeared, was stolen ... they wouldn't be barking up the wrong tree.

Rule No. 3: Temper your greed and be cool.

Of course, the temptation was to pull right up, have a friend park near the back door or just hide some stuff behind the trash container. It's there, natural to think about it. But what happens when you have the back door wide open — the UPS guy ain't there — and the boss, or one of the guys up front pops in?

"Uh, just taking out the trash?"

Really? Why aren't those boxes broken down? Wait! What's this? Do you see you're throwing out T-shirts still in their wrapper? ...is that a basketball under your sweatshirt?

No! Be cool! If you want something big you plan ahead! Start bringing in your book bag weeks in advance. Hang out around the front counter a lot before leaving. Open your bag in plane sight … pull out your car keys or school books, a CD … maybe you're just going to the food court for a meal and a study … let them think you might come back … most of all, don't let them think about that bag … just part of the outfit … a student. Be cool. Be cool … I wanted this ghetto, puffy Miami Hurricanes Starter Jacket … hood and all … I just walked right out the store with it on my back.

"This? This is *my* jacket."

No one even asked! I wore that jacket to work all winter … There's a lesson in that for you.

Right around here I got taken; worse still … I asked for it.

I was feeling good about my situation, actually saving some money — not much, but enough to see the payoff. Tracey was digging it. Fancy hotels in Philadelphia for our anniversary, cases of beer, at least 4 or 5 dime bags when I came down to visit … La Salle University, my little oasis from reality.

But my damn car! The blue Chevy Cavalier I inherited from my mom … breaking here and there! Not over heating … just broken. Get out of school one day and, shit …the fucker won't start, won't kick over. And it's not the battery! Nope. Get a jump. Go ahead. No one's stopping you.

How about coming home from class in a downpour, driving through Kearny's flooded industrial-waste wetlands. Pump the breaks! You got to! They work but the rapid decent stalls the car in knee-deep water … the only thing left to do now is roll the dice: 1, 2, 3 will dad be home?

Jack pot! Not only home, but handy Leo Alberts is around with his construction pick-up truck. They rescue me. They're going to pull me home.

"God damn piece of shit!" … that's me, all the way home … the three of us in the cab.

Of course, my dad's full of advice — probably reasonable, too. He's always good for that. But who wants to hear it? I want a new car! And I want him to pay for it … funny, huh?

As it was, my dad was paying the Cavalier's insurance … x-amount a year; after a while you tune it out. Still, I covered gas and the expenses which were piling up. Like I said, the shit was broke. Not little stuff! … new this and that. This *and* that … not one or the other … both at the same time. I was dishing it out as fast as I was making it.

Then one day my dad rolls up. There was a big excitement, my brother and sister calling me to the front of the house, to the balcony … I look down and see my dad speeding up the driveway nearly peeling out — it's steep, about 45 degrees; the contractors fucked it up. But low and behold, the most beautiful thing in the world … I could've killed that motherfucker!

Candy Apple Red. Black hardtop. Big tires … the exact one I would've picked for myself … perfect … the epitome of Jeep Wrangler.

I knew something was up right away. Dreams of driving down the shore with the top off, my board balanced in the breeze, no shirt, looking down at a car full of girls as I pass them on the Garden State Parkway … yeah, there must be a hefty price involved.

Chapter 4:

Summer Break

"If you aren't rich you should always look useful." – Louis-Ferdinand Celine

So let me tell you about my hardest job … a real dandy. This one brought to you by Leo Alberts Sr. … give thanks, give thanks. First coming to my dick's rescue — using a screwdriver to unsnap a problem I was having with a frontal wetsuit zipper … not *too* painful; the scar's not *too* big — and then this. Who could ask for more? Hookin' it up … hookin' it up … when it comes to employing the youth, elders are more than happy … O' so willing … an art! … they've made it an art!

5:00 a.m.! Bright and early … actually still dark out … "Rise n' shine … Rise n' shine … Wipe the sleepers out of your eyes." My father would've made rounds with a baton and an aluminum garbage can if he wasn't sleeping off a binge.

No time for breakfast … not even hungry … *sleepy!!!* … tired! … cranky! Anything but work! Not the mall this time … oh, no! It was summer … time to get ahead! … to bust some ass! My father wouldn't have had it any other way … Besides, a new Jeep … that's no chump change. I had a payment book: January, February, March, April, May ... all the months were represented ... $256.62! Not one year either ... it went on and on ... season tickets!

5:20 a.m. and I'm rolling up to some Spanish dude's house ... 24 going on 42 ... finished! Short, stocky ... he doesn't make me wait too long, but I get nervous anyway ... "Not on time: Early!"

Everyday the same damn thing! His girlfriend this, his girlfriend that ... they lived together with her parents ... there was a kid ... they didn't get along ... he did a lot of coke, too. Right off the passenger-side dashboard ... Bills, bitches and heartache ... I thought he was a crybaby. I didn't know yet.

Pulling up to the jobsite was not encouraging ... Trucks! Men's trucks! Trucks with toolboxes and winches ... trucks that plow snow for extra cash. Trucks with big muddy tires ... Chevies! Fords! ... patriotic ... American flags; and this well before 9/11 ... And there they were ... condominiums standing like fortresses. Their silhouettes vibrating psychedelically in the low light. You can't take your eyes off the one you inhabit ... like some god with his creation you're intimately involved.

Construction's a bitch! Very demanding. Like writing now ... too self-conscious. Your mistakes, shortcomings stare you in the face ... every crooked nail, every missed stroke of the hammer. I had no clue what was going on!

For weeks I nailed in shit here and there, set up beams, carried wood and got in peoples' way. Carrying wood was my specialty! The best in the place!

Leo would see me on site running myself stupid ... long 2 x 4s, 2 x 6s and 2 x 12s hunched over my shoulder ... I looked like a retarded helicopter ... no rotation, but I was moving nonetheless ... hovering ... kicking up dust. A compliment from him meant something ... he was a carpenter ... a specialist ... he was getting paid. Said I'm a hustler! Did you hear that? A hustler! ... Do you thank someone or punch them in the mouth?

"Oh, oh thanks … Can't stop to talk … got a bundle on my back … Thanks for noticing."

And up and down ladders all fucking day … check your fear of heights in at the door. Never mind climbing two, no, three stories … try doing it with all that lumber teetering on your back … I'm actually surprised none of us went down … me and the lumber of course … no one else was pulling that stunt … maybe the Spanish guy … but he had some marketable skills. Every now and then he'd cut out to help the surveyors … somewhere along the line he figured out how to hold that stupid stick.

But don't look passed it for a second … the wood. It's easy to. Oh, just carrying some wood from here to there. Well, from here to there is a journey. And the splinters! There's just so much of it … piles, stacks of wood. Three from that pile, four from the other and two of those on the way … "Can you toss those on for me? I can't bend over … Thanks a lot! I'm *the* hustler if you haven't heard." And off I go galloping.

The crew liked me for the most part. But this one guy, he looked like Patrick Swayze … strong, good looking … wild hair … like from Point Break … he didn't like me much … I wasn't that good. I didn't know how to nail … you reveal your level the first time you swing the hammer. I was pounding away. A tough guy! Give me a nail and I'll slam the shit out of it! … and bend it … or miss …or bend it again … what started out straight disappeared crooked into the wall.

But Point Break … he wouldn't say a thing … no encouragement … no playful jokes at my expense … he'd shake his head and get back to work, sawing, making me feel like a complete idiot … a fool … the most rudimentary things … I couldn't help it … a dunce.

He wasn't so smooth though, not by a long shot … Oh, nah, nah, nah.

What's that? You cut off half your thumb? … You don't say? … Oh … Golly. Did that hurt? … I actually asked!

Then there was Willie Nelson, what a fucking trip this guy was … always up in the rafters with his long, braided ponytail … his feet never on the ground. Don't let the glasses fool you. He'd bash ya with his Viking hammer. The "Hammer of the Gods" he called it, complete with beads, leather cord and feathers … he wasn't all peace and love.

His technique was impeccable! … *Smooth!* … Like I said, always hopping around … from one project to the next … a super specialist … he worked alone … solving problems … starting major projects we'd back him up on but only after he decided the angles, set a base … and then off he went again, somewhere else … usually higher up … a real monkey. Never a dropped nail! Tape measure, chalk line: always in check. He thought he could run the operation and probably could.

But the boss! The boss was something else entirely… Upstate Hippie Redneck! No doubt about that … also with the braided po nytail. Except not Norwegian blond … pissed off red-Irish! I knew he went to Vietnam without asking. He had a military countenance … not an all-tidy, peacetime, volunteer, work-your-way-up disciplined officer … no, not at all …more, I'll cut your fucking throat been through hand-to-hand combat in some fucking overrun jungle outpost draftee … someone who saw too much … got more than his money's worth. He knew his shit … no one could deny it. A nice guy! Real cool! Patient with my skill-less ass; always in amongst us … his hammer wasn't collecting dust. But whether he liked it or not, Boss Man was establishment on this hippie crew … he was a constructionist, a builder. An object had to be built by such and such a time … all their money counted on it. Run over the date? Cut into profits! These guys were living away from their families, all piled into a rented house a few miles away in Clifton, New Jersey. This was a major project; a mini neighborhood of town houses … who knows how much they'd pocket if all goes well. They weren't telling me.

———∼∽∼———

At times I'm surprised the whole kit-and-caboodle didn't come down on our heads … not like those guys weren't smoking enough dope. Me? I wasn't invited. I had to settle for tuna-fish sandwiches and Gatorade; drag my ass to the coffee truck and burrow back into the shadows of our timber-framed fortress … anything to get out of the sun.

The radio made it real clear: "Stay indoors!" … "Record heat!" … "Avoid all strenuous activities" … "Drink lots of water!" … "Alert! Alert! Alert!"

Us? We're on the roof! No shirts. No hardhats. Balancing on 2 x 12s three stories up … the 2" was your surface area.; your footing. It was more like monkey bars than a roof … we were working on it. My job was to nail in the buttresses … should make ya want to give your house a once over.

From way up there I spotted Mark strolling into the complex around noon … lunch was over. We tended to break early … the coffee truck would show up by 10:30 and we'd already be starving, tired … too tired for exclamation points. We worked through sunrise; the morning dew revealing the lumber's true nature … our hands sticky, sappy from resin, nicked, dented, swollen. All the good guys wore gloves … took me a couple weeks to learn, to catch on … I can be oblivious sometimes … part of my nature … a little carefree.

"Splinters? Ah, whatever" … Yeah, until you get a 2-inch fragment lodged in the soft meat between your thumb and forefinger. That will wizen you up.

Personally, I couldn't stand Mark surfing all summer without me. He had just gotten fired from yet another restaurant so now it was now my turn to hook him up! … all those waiters do is drink and coke … a full on catered party, the restaurant business. I wouldn't stand for it. "Steady work, Mark! Steady work! … Good pay! … $12 an hour."

It's tempting! I was tan and pretty buff … the wood … it's not light.

I called down to him … I felt cool as shit standing up there on the edge of the roof … shirtless, cut off beige denim slacks … work belt … my hammer holstered … casual … hitting the water bottle, wiping off some sweat … gazing over the scenery … the height! … the height! … majestic on my fortress!

Then there was Mark: total rookie! I know; I've been there … jeans, sneakers and a collared Rugby shirt … He must not have been listening … The heat! The lifting! The resin! … Nobody listens … The pot smoking! Didn't he hear? Nobody would care about his starched collar … Got a hammer? Some nails? Water? … "Nope." "Nope." "Nope." … Well then what good are ya? … Go back to the playground, kid … go back to fast-pitch stick ball … the spray-painted boxes … we got work to do … we're building homes … fortifications of the American dream.

It didn't matter … 4:00 p.m.: no sign of Mark! I was thinking about grabbing a beer, at the very least a dip in the pool, some BBQ chicken. My dad was turning into a real Betty Crocker … being home by dinner and pouring BBQ sauce over the grill became his thing … I wasn't going to complain.

I called Mark when I got home. He told me he left! Walked right off the job!

… Was that legal?

… I wanted to play by those rules!

That guy left jobs like I walked away from empty dinner tables. Then again, he wasn't walking around with $256.62 stamped on his ass … hell's bells! His folks bought him that used Firebird … the one he turned into a golf ball squeezing by the garbage truck … faded black … stick shift … real cool … he taught me how to drive my Jeep … that it's all in the clutch … easing it.

Turned out the kid actually had it easy. His assignment? … Finishing! … Hell, he could've kept the Rugby shirt on … no sweat … indoors all day! In the shade! NO LIFTING! Put a door in here

… a windowsill there … maybe a mailbox. Thing is, he worked with a know-it-all … by his side every second … riding him.

"But Mark … they're all know-it-alls! He's your boss."

Didn't matter! He didn't wait around. Told the guy to fuck off and away he went … I actually saw him walking off site … I thought they sent him on a chore … it was still early, maybe 1:00 … he skeddadled before he could get dirty. I can't blame him … if I didn't have $256.62 tattooed to my ass … "Sleeping in! Don't forget to turn off the lights! Close the door."

All my other friends? Ah, the summer! To shore houses! Line them up … beer kegs, drunken boardwalk strolls, you name it. Tracey off to Europe how nice … Italy, Switzerland, Germany, Amsterdam! Brought me back a T-shirt from The Bulldog Coffee Shop … she wasn't bragging about their coffee! … Oh, no! And hostels here and hostels there … cross-continental train rides just for the fun of it … I wondered about the dick … did she develop an international palate? … I didn't broach the subject, but like I said, I sure did wonder.

❧

It wasn't a happy place … not by far. A lot of guys away from their families … a lot of guys divorced, bitching about alimony … most on drugs, one sort or another — some pretty much on everything. One guy, a junkie, he fell two stories and broke his back … upset the whole place … drooping heads everywhere … it really affected morale. I wasn't too disturbed or shocked the way these guys pranced around up there. Me? I shimmied on my ass; I can admit it … three stories up on a Swish-cheese roof … big open sections you can look down into and see Willie Nelson with his hammer below in the shade.

But the rooftop in July … definitely a job for Patrick Swayze and Ray.

I have to say, they gave me a chance! They tried setting me up at the cutting horse below, ground level — in the shade most of the afternoon – but I couldn't handle the coordinates:

"Triangle piece! 48 x 17 x 32!"

What the hell did that mean? What kind of screwy triangle is that? What wood? What saw? Is this thing plugged in? What about my fingers? Yeah, I had all kinds of questions … I stood there dumb-founded. Swayze wanted to come down and show me himself … it was something he learned to love. Big Boss-man wouldn't have it … he needed someone experienced on the roof or we'd be there to sun-down … it happened every now and then. I hated it! I wasn't getting the overtime these guys were getting and, unlike them, I had some pussy to get home to. End of season, Tracey was back from Europe with countless stories … over and over … you know how women are … here and there … and here and there again but with a new twist … maybe a mention of "some guys they met." Blah, blah, blah, blah, blah … just blow me already! I'm tired. Been working hard all day.

So, this is how it was day in and day out. The only time I ever got yelled at — and believe me, you don't want one of these guys in your face — was when I got hurt.

Our townhouse was done. Detail crews were still putting up alu-minum siding and doorknobs — full on bells and whistles — but our job was complete; we built the fucker. Now we moved on to the next lot which was nothing more than a gray cement slab … I tried to envision an air-conditioning unit here, a garage entrance there … then we broke out the chalk lines.

How I loved to snap chalk! Willie Nelson and Patrick Swayze would measure it all out … great mathematicians! Find me someone dealing with fractions everyday like these guys: "Two and three quar-ters" here … "Seven and four sixteenths" over there … real fucking wizards, virtual Steven Hawkins. I'd stretch out my chalk line from red-pencil "x" to red pencil "x" … sometimes it was way over there … a great distance … I'd have to drive a cement nail down to hold one end in place and take the whole pocket-sized concoction for a walk … like measuring a First Down … once the line was taught: give it a snap … I was amazed the first time. Ingenious! The entire string vibrates like a giant guitar and the blur's intensified by an explosion of chalk dust … if you'd taken a picture of my face the first time … flabbergasted! … Egyptian, they said. The technology. I think.

So, we marked the shit out of this foundation … pink lines everywhere. I don't understand the pink. Is there a need? Why not green? Are there other colors? Was this just some rookie stunt? Hazing? Or is it me? Do I have a hang up? Anyway, a big truck drops off a container and naturally I begin to get nervous … I wasn't sporting any underwear … the last few days had been light … popping lines here and there … a joke … a breeze … that would've been the time to spark up, oh yes indeed. But out of the blue, a container! But different then the ones I'm used to … a convertible! That's right … no fucking roof. And then all hell breaks loose … people all over the compound start clearing out … driving their trucks away … picking up their valuables and skedaddling! … The earth was shaking … I could hear and feel a large mechanism approaching.

I couldn't quite put it all together. A crane? You mean we're not going to lift this shit ourselves? … I felt lazy … for the first time in my life, not the mule, not the one in the pit … I didn't know what to do. I tightened my work belt anyway … out of habit … surely something had to be carried and I had a good idea who'd be doing it.

But it never happened. In fact, it was the Spanish dude who hit the truck … and even in there it wasn't bad. He just strapped what looked like a flat fire hose around wooden frames … that was it … Tally Ho! … Up, Up and Away … a 500lb wall frame flying overhead … "Did it ever fall?" … I was a little safety conscious … always have been … They assured me: "Never!"

As long as I wasn't lifting shit, I wasn't about to complain … You can Up, Up and Away all day long … Our job: Balance the walls on their way down; guide them to their corresponding numbered chalk line. As soon as that happened … bang, bang, bang … nail them right into place. And then another one … and then another … in no time flat the place was starting to shape up. Things were going so well; we were so glad to be off the roof and drunk from a week of chalk snapping … we decided to take off our hardhats and enjoy the nice day … yup … And then one of those walls came crashing down right on my head! … *boop!!!* … goodnight … not all the way! … just to the verge! Like when I've been hit a few times playing ball or fighting … dropped right to a single knee, head down. "Just need a minute … Give me a second."

It must have looked pretty bad. Even Swayze stopped what he was doing and signaled to the crane to hold up the works … Spanish dude poked his head out from the container … Big Boss-man and Willie Nelson were right there, right by my side. They helped me up, just for morale's sake, and then put me back down in a corner. How did I feel? Could I see? How many fingers? Boy were they concerned … there was some blood.

Should I go home? It was offered.

I start calculating: it's already 4:00 p.m. … it can't be much longer. I thought I'd stick it out … had nothing to do with the $256.62 — not even a thought at the time. The decision was fueled from somewhere in the core of my manhood … Tough! Got to be! These were all men and I was on the verge … would've been long drafted and shot up back in the day … no, I'd hang in there.

As soon as I proved OK and stupid enough to stay Big Boss-man let us have it; though he didn't single me out:

"What the fuck are you guys doing without your hats?" … "Why wasn't that wall nailed down? How do you walk away from a wall without putting a fucking nail in it!"

It all seemed so rudimentary from my dazed perspective … Who didn't nail down that wall? I knew it wasn't my wall, that's how it got me from behind. Boss-man wasn't around and Willie, Willie was faultless on the job, a magician. I wonder who it could've been.

I don't know about you, but I'd rather have a cautious hustler on my crew capable of learning than a construction prodigy who is good for a slip up every few years … yesterday his little piggy, today my skull, tomorrow your balls … fucking Swayze.

Chapter 5:

——— ∽ ———

BACK AT THE MALL

"Woe to those who call evil good and good evil, who put darkness for light and light for darkness. — Isaiah, 5:20

There're no breaks, no "Take it easy" … Hell no! Forget it!

School? Are you kidding me? … pussy shit! … a vacation! That's what my father would have you believe. He didn't want to hear about Spanish exams. Spanish exams? … I should've had that shit wired years ago; wasn't I paying attention? … Him … Abuela … My American mother … real white bred … if she could learn it why couldn't I? It's not so hard … "Spanish is the easiest language!" … Yeah … maybe … if you give a fuck.

Calculus? I can hear him in the back of my mind: "2 + 2 = 4 … add it up!" … felt like a damn slacker for not understanding. Up all night cramming: earn a big 1.5 on the mid-term … eanie, meanie, miny, mo … pick an answer. Didn't matter it wasn't multiple choice; any number would do … circle it. Show some work. A big 360 right around a made-up number.

I wasn't doing so well. I wasn't studying much either.

Balance.

On one side: Economics, History, English Lit. On the other: Spanish, Calculus … guess which side was suffering?

I was a fucking Lee Iacoka in economics class. Are you kidding me? Guns-n-Butter? … Common fucking sense! Street smarts 101! … I got what ya want and there ain't a lot of it: cha-fucking-ching … or … the shit's as plentiful as Newark-night smog … Well, trust me, my shit's a little better … and it's five bucks less … real hush hush … just take it and be on your way … remember … not a word … let's just keep it between us now, heh?

Yeah, I understood the marketing side before we got to it. I've been putting a pretty face on shit for a long time … covering up real disasters. My parents didn't hear the half of it and neither will you.

⌘

We were heading home through South Kearny, the swamps. Over the same dilapidated bridge featured in the introduction of The Sopranos. Past the jail. Past the oil refineries and the two mountains of garbage. If you got lost, somehow found yourself in this armpit of New Jersey, you might think it's a park for these poor ghetto bastards … you'd be wrong. It's toxic sludge brought in from across the nation covered with grass and scrub brush … a half-assed attempt at camouflage. But it's not necessary. The locals don't even consider it … just a decoration on the drive to Jersey City; something to look at coming out of the Lincoln Tunnel.

It was a long night in New York City with fake IDs and somebody in the back seat flashed the van behind us the middle finger … what a childish, stupid thing to do. You never know who the other guy, or in this case, guys could be.

These guys were the type of guys that followed us to Stewart's, the drive up fast-food and Root Beer joint where Mark waitered and stashed his car for the night. Now it was early, about 4:30 in the morning and there was no one around.

So here come the headlights. And they're coming in aggressively … we knew it was trouble parked in the corner in Richie's Montero, our bullshit session shattered by the dread and panic of imminent physical danger. The energy transcended bloody noses and broken teeth; it was lethal.

Mark made a run for his Firebird. I was praying it would kick over because it could be temperamental, especially the way Mark bounced it around. He really played ping-pong with that thing … he was on his own now and that didn't bode well for anyone except the three or four guys filing out of the van's sliding door.

Mark hasn't had good luck. He caught a beating while drinking beers and eating mescaline with his preppy gringo friends at the abandoned docks in Jersey City. A raging, jealous boyfriend popped out of a car in a case of mistaken identity and laid down the law with a pipe. Mark got rushed to the hospital for plastic surgery while tripping face.

Thank God the Firebird starts up and he's out. Like Flash Gordon! That boy was gone.

I don't know why I had a knife, but I did. Because I remember thinking, if this motherfucker banging on the glass breaks through, I'm going to give it to him in his arm.

Richie had the good sense to get the hell out of there without worrying about blinkers and fastening safety belts. He clipped one guy hanging onto the hood … like a monkey at Great Adventure. *Thump.*

There's another guy in the van loading a shotgun. I see him feeding shells into the chamber as we pull out of the parking lot. He's anxious. He can't wait … we're easy prey getting away.

We drive straight to the North Arlington police department! No red lights. No stop signs. We want to get pulled over. A confrontation with the police is exactly what we're looking for.

We didn't consider the damage the Montero might have taken or if a shoe had been inadvertently stuck in the grill. Maybe that's why they weren't behind us? Perhaps the hood clutcher wound up with a Donald Duck foot. Super flat. Maybe he was a little wobbly from the waist down?

Either way, Richie didn't want to drop me off and go home alone. I didn't blame him. His side of the neighborhood could get rough as it is … following him home, watching the sun cast the day's first pink rays of light on downtown Newark's mini-skyscrapers, I thought about how ludicrous life had become since my mom died. And how I was going to have to fight to hold onto the good inside of me.

There's no cool way to say it, so I'll come right out with it: My ass wound up back at the mall. Not like I wanted it to, but $256.62 … there's no escaping it. After a few months on the lamb — surfing and adjusting to a college schedule — it was time to go back to work. What's more, Christmas was around the corner. Tracey would be expecting something.

But this new job, Banana-fucking-Republic, boy was that place something else … not a particularly spectacular stop in the big scheme of things when compared to UPS, 5:00 a.m. construction mornings and covert CHAMP embezzlement schemes. Nevertheless, I learned a thing or two.

First off: the whole operation owned by the GAP … and Jesus Christ was that place uptight. First day in the door: "Pick out some outfits. You need to be in our clothes while on the sale's floor."

OK, great, a uniform. But everything is so Goddamn expensive … shirts, ties, jeans … everything's over $150. Upscale and classy

… Not my salary though! They definitely got me on the cheep! Mall wages! $5.50 an hour or something ridiculous like that. A cut in pay … got to say it. But remind the ladies: I'm not a loser … I was doing all right 'til then. Brand new Jeep! Let's not forget that! The mailman didn't … every month … little envelops to be returned with my obligation: $256.62.

Want to know what Banana Republic is really crazy about? Fucking hangers!!! As essential the box is to UPS, hangers are to Banana Republic … how's that for an SAT simile? These people were fanatics! Three-quarters of my time was spent spacing hangers out evenly across their racks. Evenly! No exceptions! Getting all up in there … millimeters to the right … millimeters to the left. Sometimes a shipment would come in and the rack would be full … 10, 15 hangers … real tight. The epitome of precision! The best? Three to four jackets! Easy to space! Plenty of room to breathe. You think I'm joking? Go look! I guarantee it. And if they're not evenly spaced someone's slacking … they'll hear about it … believe me.

But you don't care about any of this and frankly, I don't care to write about it … the whole operation was stuffy. No stealing! No way! They checked your bag on the way out: it was store policy; managers weren't exempt … even the fine ass boss. She wore thongs under her overpriced tight khakis. I can't remember her name, but I remember her ass! Side to side — swish, swish — real sweet.

CHAPTER 6:

SLICE OF HEAVEN AND HELL

"Three things cannot be long hidden: the sun, the moon, and the truth."—Buddha

Some jobs are better than others … no doubt about it. Take Banana Republic: You didn't see me running off at the mouth over that, did ya? What? Three pages! And that's with mentioning the boss' ass. But a few that I've found … real gems! Couldn't be me without them.

Standing in front of Banana Republic dressed like a dork hounding people … "Can I help you? Can I help you?" … it just wasn't me; not even close. I'd just as soon give ya the keys to the joint, "Help yourself to some overpriced shit."

Their clothes lasted though; I'll give them that. I still got a linen shirt … real nice but wrinkled as fuck. I hang it in the bathroom while running the shower full blast … steam the whole joint up … doesn't matter: wrinkled! I got a blue blazer, too … real, real nice … $550 before the employee discount.

42

I got to wear it on my next interview.

Guess where?

Back at UPS! Back at the human resources department in Secaucus.

But don't go getting any funny ideas … forget carrying the boxes!!! … This time my reputation preceded me. I was a dignitary of St. Peters College.

With neither my knowledge nor consent the business department finagled me an interview for a paid internship. And to make matters worse, my father intercepted the postcard announcing the appointment. That didn't leave much room for discussion.

"Have you ever done sales?"

Have I done sales? I've bothered the shit out of a whole bunch of people up in that mall. I wouldn't exactly say "selling." I mean, nobody walked out with anything they didn't want, picked off the rack themselves or asked for by name … but I handed it to them … I pointed to the register.

No need to tell them that though. And while I'm being less than truthful, lets tell them I did sales at CHAMPS too; my uncle would vouch for me … aside from a few suspicious glances I'm quite sure he didn't suspect me of embezzlement.

They also wanted to know if I had a car.

Did I!

If it wasn't for that fucking thing, I wouldn't have been there in the first place.

You should have seen his face when I told him I had a brand-new Jeep. He was downright discontented. Like he had shit in his pants.

He must've thought I was some pretty rich boy cashing in on one of daddy's favors … If he only knew. Dad was back home and headed for Pluto … 3, 2, 1: ready for blast off (*snort*)!

Get out of school 'bout noon — all early classes, starting at 8:00 a.m. — and book ass up Kennedy Blvd. When I hit Route 3: no skittdadling, straight to UPS' Secaucus compound. Already running late! Intern or not, student or no student, they would've had me there fist thing in the morning … management wasn't exactly pro scholastic.

Empty your pockets and flash the security guard your I.D.; wait for everything to plop off the conveyor on the other side and hoof it past the hollow containers lined to infinity across the black-asphalt parking lot. Say hello to a few heads (don't be rude) … some truckers, some loaders, some VIP executives who are "bosses" somewhere up the chain of command. They look out of place, foolish in their jackets and ties … me too. Dressed to the T amid all this hard work; we're obviously involved in the pussy end of the business.

Once inside the HUB … there's the brown vans … you can't miss them. The entire operation takes place in what amounts to a huge airplane hanger. Look up: conveyor belts and beams supporting more conveyor belts everywhere … just like South Orange only bigger. Everything's painted UPS brown except a yellow line on the gray floor leading you to a far-off staircase and shabby basement offices.

From there I fax my timesheet to another UPS office about three blocks away — those folks want to be completely removed, they don't even want to see a box … then I hop back into the Jeep and head to any number of destinations within my territory: East Orange; West Orange; South Orange … their ain't a North Orange … Kearny, my home town; Harrison; Woodridge; Little Falls; Hackensack; and sometimes Newark. Any given day: any town … up to me.

I knew what they wanted me to do: follow leads and establish new customers, give them UPS ID numbers and supplies so they could begin shipping with us. And I did that sometimes. But usually I'd encounter offices that already had UPS accounts and I'd just give them new ID numbers — numbers that could be tracked and their business credited to me. Though there were times when I'd run into a secretary hiding behind the glass, like at a doctor's office, and actually make a sale. They wouldn't be using UPS; they'd be all about the FedEx.

"Well, FedEx is $13.95 but we provide the same next-day service for $11. All you have to do is take some of these envelopes and this ID card. Just drop it in the box downstairs. There's no other charge. We'll simply bill you … you're saving three dollars every time."

It was an easy sell. Sometimes I wouldn't even ask. You come into a place claiming UPS and they think you're with the government. Hell, sometimes I'd double park and put my UPS ID on the dashboard … never a problem! I'd hand a whole stack of envelopes over to the lady with her face pressed up against the glass, sliding them through the slot like some inmate's meal. They'd take 'em. I'd track 'em. Sure enough, about two weeks later I start getting credit for the activity — doesn't matter that someone else already opened an account with them … they have a new number now: my number.

That's what I was kind of supposed to be doing. This is what I did:

Blow off my last class and boogie out of there by 10:50 a.m. … 10:50! Not 11:00! … Run to the Arab deli on the corner; grab a sandwich — a man's got to eat — and fax my timesheet in from there … they charge $0.75 … it's worth it. From there kick ass straight home! No fucking around! No stopping or slowing on yellow! Certainly pass on the right if required … the shoulder is your friend. Once home: grab my board and twist a few joints for good measure and be on my way.

Of course, my dad warned me not to press my luck … was the natural thing to do. "Son," he'd say, "you're making good money and working from your car. Don't blow this."

What he failed to realize was that the real jeopardy was in blowing the internship, letting St. Peters down. I was earning three credits for that gig and if I got fired, well, I would assume that would be deemed "unsatisfactory."

It didn't really matter to me though … *"This surf session brought to you by UPS!"* I should've been upfront with them and just painted their logo on my board; at least let them get some advertising out of it. At that stage I spent most of my time underwater, the board popping up in the air. It would've been good for a few laughs.

Winter, Spring, Summer, Fall … I was there: chest deep floating beside the Manasquan inlet … huge boulders, massive. At least 100 yards long, 15- to 20 wide …an array of fishermen casting into our midst. And don't let that "Winter" pass you by. Real easy to in that group: "Winter, Spring, Summer, Fall." Sounds like a commercial for Vermont … No! Think 33-degree water! I say 33 only because it wasn't frozen. But a few times it was … actual icebergs floating in the saltwater lineup.

And yeah, yeah with the wetsuit … I know how you think … it keeps ya warm. Same way a blanket would in February if ya laid down for a nap in Central Park … it's something, it's helping out. But when a big set starts feathering on the horizon and you're caught inside … when it bounces off that jetty and doubles up … no way of making it over … it's your face that's leading the charge under it. And at 8- to 10 feet — you can't get deep enough with a wetsuit's buoyancy — that's a lot of cold, heavy water coming down on your head. A few times I drove all the way down there and forgot my hood! One hour each way … but when you're young and crazy and say the cold won't kill you it doesn't.

⁓

I have to interject for a moment. Forgive me. You're receiving this message from the future … orders from my maybe-so literary agent. She says I'm too harsh on women. That I should write more about my mother, that it will help clarify my relationships.

Maybe she's right. I'm not sure if you can tell yet, but I kind of breeze through. I cast with a wide net. I don't like to dilly-dally and draw things out and I'm not one for the boo hoos.

Truth is, I thought I was done with this book 10 years ago. I thought I could get away with it. Amaze you with my dot dot dots.

My chaste wife agrees with her. You'll see. Just be patient. She's convinced we can't move far enough once people read this book. That I'll offend everyone … Lets pray. I like my space.

But let's get back on track. We're here for a reason. I'm not sitting here writing this for my health. I don't want to have to go through this again.

I set out to go surfing and for some reason — maybe it was late in the day and the Turnpike was backed up — I double back.

I try to park out front but can't. My neighbor across the street has a penchant for banging a u-ey and taking my spot. He likes to save his space for when his son comes to visit.

I'm definitely not happy. I'm schlepping my board, wetsuit and backpack from way down the block.

I finally reach the house, the steep Mount Everest driveway. I dish the dry wetsuit in the basement, traverse the stairs and open the kitchen door to a feast…. A verifiable party. The joke was on me.

My sister, who had cleared out with her boyfriend months ago, had returned. She had graduated college and was about to get married. My brother Chris was there, too…. and so was the woman my father was dating while my mother was dying … feeding her fat face in my mother's chair.

My dad needed to adjust his cocaine dosage. Ease it back or double it. Triple it. Or get a new vendor … His eyes were playing tricks on him. His mind wasn't serving him well … talk about a downgrade.

I surprised everybody real good. Caught them completely unexpected. They were wise not to invite me … I was tempted to pull a Jesus in the Temple act. Start flipping shit over. But when you're young and dependent you have to put on a happy face. You have to smile at the enemy. But I knew, somehow I'd have to break away real soon.

I stuck to my routine: school, surf, work, smoke weed whenever I could. Keep it simple. Try to stay numb. The dreams of my mother walking though the door had subsided.

My sister was worried about leaving me and my brother behind. We understood. She had it harder than us. My father expected her to fill in for my mother. He ranted and raved at my aunts who were spitting images of my mom. He did his best to keep everyone away. And succeeded.

I couldn't understand how my mom's family abandoned us. We were used to three square meals a day. My brother was still getting tucked in at night ... if it wasn't for Abuela, me and my brother would've been Lord of the Flies; eating roadkill and wiping our asses with our hands.

We planned an intervention. Me, my brother and sister ... we knock on our dad's bedroom door... we didn't like going in that room.

We wake him up. He just got home ... We beg. We plead. We're all crying. We're trying to make him understand we're essentially orphans now. To have mercy on us.

He gets up. He rants and raves. It's his specialty. Starts breaking what's left of the glass mirror on the overhead canopy of his marital bed ... It didn't go too well. He disappears for another week. No sight or sound. He's playing hide-and-go-seek with us.

The night he gets back, I'm in my bedroom getting ready to go out. I have the music turned up. I'm purposely playing the Grateful Dead's Casey Jones ... *"Driving that train, high on cocaine."* ... I know he doesn't like it. He's mentioned it ... fuck him!

I hear something. I turn the music down.

There it goes again.

I walk over to my father's dreaded bedroom door. I sneak a peek … nobody's home. He must have gone out again.

I turn the music back up. I get brazen. Instead of twisting joints in the bathroom I get comfortable, set to work at this very same writing desk.

There it is again. Some shuffling … I know Abuela ain't so heavy footed. She likes to sneak up. Just appear. Always trying to catch you in the act.

I go back to the master bedroom. Peek my head in a little deeper.

Aha! I see a light trickling out from under the bathroom door.

I'm going to take a play out of Abuela's handbook and arrive on the scene. I want to catch him putting shit up his nose.

I open the door. It's not what I expected. Foolishly never considered it … he's hanging himself with a belt from the shower faucet. His face is purple and swollen with blood. It looks like a water balloon about to burst. Snot's squeezing out of his nose.

It's taken me many years to reconcile lifting his body up, removing the belt. For a long time I felt we would've all been better served if I just closed the door; quietly walked away.

PART II:

ASCENDING NOWHERE

CHAPTER 7:

VICTORIOUS LOSER

"Call unto me, and I will answer thee, and show thee great and mighty things, which thou knowest not." — *Jeremiah 33:3*

I can admit it: I cheated; the pussy overlapped. Not like I didn't warn her … Tracey, who was having more than her fair share of fun.

My mom?

… her dead body wasn't even cold yet.

My dad?

… hell, your guess is as good as mine … maybe at Pepe's after-hours club. Maybe surrounded by coke whores. Maybe he's in his new Lexus wrapped around a tree … well, not yet. But events were certainly leading up to it … believe me; it was obvious. It didn't take Nostradamus. I didn't have to summon Edgar Casey.

And where's Waldo? Where's my girlfriend?

Fuck, she's off to college, cotton candy land. Kissing rich frat boys in Philly.

But don't cry for me Argentina. Oh no. If there's one thing in my DNA ... Quiet rage! Rebellion. Retribution ... sad sorrowful lamentations of self-destruction. High yet so low in nightclub corners.

I met Maria at a hardcore punk show way up Route 17, past Ramapo, where there's forests, clean air, parks, nice cars, lots of white people. It's not somewhere we would've gone on our own but a Portuguese buddy from Newark finagled a sort of half date with a couple girls he knew from St. Johns.

I ran into Maria on the stairwell between the bar and bathroom. She was a little big in the caboose but not fat! At least that was the first impression with her frumpy "alternative" clothes ... it was the times ... Pearl Jam ... Alice In Chains ... Nirvana.

Totally misleading!!!

Take it all off ... Perfect 10! ... ideal female form! ... hourglass! ... in a tight 24-year-old package! I was out of my under-age league.

The thing with Maria, however, is that she couldn't cum.

I know! I know! *You could make her do it!* You'd go down on her for an hour ... nice and soft, teasing. Or, if that don't work, you'll start working a finger in, start lapping up the clit real good. Or sit her on your cock, nice and stiff ... squeeze that ass, suck those tits ... roll her over and nibble on her neck as ya tell her how good it feels from behind. I know! I tried it all! I took her camping and went down on her till my mouth was numb ... no dice! ... I lasted longer than the fire. One eye on the smoldering coals, one on the task at hand.

Of course, I had no problems in that department myself; and boy did she go out of her way. She'd sprawl me out on her bed, her widowed mom downstairs, and give me a back rub to die for. Get me all oiled up ... candles, incense, aromatherapy gels ... the whole shebang. She was officially studying Shiatsu and, from the looks of her bookshelf, knew a thing or two about reflexology.

Lots of times I'd fall asleep. Who wouldn't? Most of the time she'd roll me over and suck me off. Not the best I've had, but pretty damn special nonetheless ... She was a spitter ... should make that distinction. But at 20 this was all very much OK with me.

There was more to Maria than kneading hands and a dreamy mouth; she was also abandoning a hell of a job. You'd have to be a surfer, stoner or complete space cadet to understand, but I had an opportunity to give up a paid internship with tons of potential to slide into her slot at a head shop selling tie-dyed T-shirts, candles, incense ... all kinds of hippie crap.

My dad thought I was fucking nuts ... I have to give it to him. After all, I was getting paid well to do absolutely nothing at UPS. To go surf. And I must have sounded fucking nuts when I listed my hair as a primary factor. Sounds silly; I know. But frankly I was tired of sporting a suit to school and jelling my hair so it would stay above the collar.

Now I could get stoned at work! And of course, this was the appeal. It wasn't exactly sanctioned, mind you — but we found ways ... basically whenever Jill, the Deadhead but sober vegan manager stepped out. The method wasn't elaborate: always in the bathroom, sometimes with a spoof and always with incense ... we had more than enough to spare.

Native Art's other appeal was that it was constantly packed with pussy! Real cute American girls who were always stoned or pretending to be ... I'd drive myself crazy checking them out in their backless shirts. They'd come in for everything ... for balls of hemp ... for rings ... for patches ... for lava lamps and black lights ... sometimes just to say hello.

Not to brag, but the degree to which this pussy presented itself: staggering! Not to be seen again for some time. The rate at which I turned away from it: nothing short of moronic!!!

Jill was out of the question. She was the boss; enough said. Her body was dope … real tight for her age, about 28. But it was all the "Ray, can ya straighten this out?" … "Ray, can ya straighten that out?" … "Ray, can ya do a handstand while I light a stick of patchouli up your ass?"

She was determined. The place was to look like the inside of a 1969 Volkswagen at all times. But well kept. Everything in its right place … well, mostly anyway.

Kerri on the other hand, the associate manager, she was something else altogether. A total coke whore! Now, she wasn't technically a whore; but boy did she like coke and dick. One up her nose, the other up her snatch.

A total standout in any crowd; the desire for sex emanated from her. You could smell it. It was a constant taunt amplified by its confirmed availability. Icelandic, she was female confidence personified … I was a little boy.

A bunch of us would go back to her place after work (not Jill) and she would strip. Just her top, but down to the titties … cute little perky things. I'd get up to pour myself another drink and maybe, just maybe, I'd go so far as to do a body shot … but off her neck; and making sure never to get caught gazing at her tits.

One night after work, we both head back to her place for a little pre-night-out action. By this time, she was tired of my dead-end flirting; I'd take it so far, suggest that I was interested, but when it was put on the plate, I'd back away … this night was going to be different.

Right off the bat: straight vodka down … twice! … three times! … and then hit the shower solo. I was hoping she'd come in and flirt, it was her way … Nope. She must have really been fed up with my ass.

Walk out in my towel … still nothing.

Pour another drink, chase it with a beer, smoke a joint ... nothing, nothing, nothing ... she's almost completely dressed and her boyfriend's waiting for us at the cokehead lounge ... they know the owner.

I had enough. Laying back on her bed I stuck out my legs and jiu-jitsu scissor swept her, I drew her in. The move was unprecedented! She shot me a look as if to ask, "Are you going to do something this time or sit there with a limp dick?"

I dove in! I remember her red jeans. I remember being overly aggressive as I went down on her; I flipped us both over and now she was on the bed and I was kneeling before her. I remember munching, actually digging in there with my entire mouth. She got into it quicker than I anticipated ... she rolled me over! Her cold hand (she had been drinking a beer) shot down my pants. I remember feeling a number of her rings ... none of them pleasant.

I wanted a blowjob. I arched my back thrusting my cock upwards beckoning ... she wasn't having it.

I don't remember why I didn't fuck her. She asked me too. I said something about condoms, not having them ... No sweat! She pulled out a smorgasbord from her sock drawer. She was fully stocked! I didn't know what to say. I think I might have actually requested head.

Big mistake! She got up and dressed. It was time to go.

It didn't take me much longer than following her to the club (trying to keep it together) to replay the entire night through my mind the way it should've went down: Fuck the condom! I should've stuck it right in and banged the shit out of her. I should've pulled out last minute, looked her right in the eye and cum all over her tummy: "Good night! See ya at work tomorrow."

Instead I got wasted, watched her hang on her boyfriend till the sun came up and prayed my way home to an empty, quiet house.

<div align="center">~~~</div>

Brenda definitely liked to drink; she'd come in feeling real good. So good in fact her and Jill had a few sit-downs … nothing serious, but backroom stuff. "Don't tell anyone but Brenda has a drinking problem."

"Oh, OK … sure thing Jill."

I decided it best not to mention the bags of coke she was snorting … if Jill thinks she's hitting the bar for an hour or two before work so be it … Who does it hurt? Of course, there was the reality of the matter: she's really coming in from Kerri's … the super after-hours party! Ultra fucked up! … so fucked up it's the exhaustion tremors; millions of mini ones that no one can see but they're there.

Fucking girl was definitely my type though. Super tight body … a real Puerto Rican island-style import. Not some gold-tooth bitch with a box cutter.

Normally I don't mess with Hispanic chicks, just as a rule. They're either virgins praying to the Lady Fattima in front of their house or too much attitude. Either way, they have an 85 percent chance of acquiring an *arros con pollo* ass … consider yourself warned.

Brenda was in no danger though, at least no time soon. And I was certainly committed to getting some of that.

Sounds real cool and calculated, right? Well, let me explain it to you so you get it straight:

It was a ridiculous snowstorm … four feet had already fallen and there were reports of double-digit snowdrifts. Brenda usually took the bus … two hours each way! You won't get that out of an American girl, no fucking way! So, when she asked for a ride, something she's never done before, I couldn't say no … the conditions certainly warranted it. So, into the Jeep we go. (I had a Shakespeare final the next day … *Blow, blow, thou winter wind* … You could say that again!)

Route 46 was a winter wonderland. The snow's coming down so fast that the few cars on the road are leaving no tracks.

"Ray, this isn't my normal bus route." … that's Brenda trying to justify that she doesn't know how to get home.

Somehow, we find her exit. Blocking the off ramp is an old Ford that has spun 180 degrees and shining us with its headlights. The guy needs help. He's no spring chicken … I hop out … push, push, push … no traction. Back into the Jeep I go … I ease up to his fender … a little gas … a little more gas … in no time we're all on our way again.

There's Brenda's bar! *Now* she knows where she is. The guessing game is over.

We might as well. I mean, it's not like the snow isn't just going to get deeper … we laugh about it over some drinks.

I finally reach that point; I'm wasted. If I have two more beers I'll probably puke, maybe fall down. It's definitely time to go. I kick out the mound of snow that's accumulated under my Jeep … it's piled about a foot-and-a-half thick on my windshield. Yeah, this is going to be fun. At least I'll have an excuse for swerving.

The chariot finally arrives; we roll up to Brenda's house … it's a three family. My money is she's on the second or third floor; I doubt she and her family are homeowners. I also doubt she'll pull away if I kiss her … I think of her boyfriend (damn!), I think about her soon becoming a manager, another boss; standing next to her on Saturday mornings: "What'd ya do last night?"

She interrupts my pathetic thoughts. "Why don't we get a hotel room? We can split it."

It's right here that I blow it again. Take account.

"I can't. I'm saving for Costa Rica." (Don't worry; you'll hear about this hair-brain fiasco … a real gem.)

She says she'll pay for the room outright! I guess she got the raise already … more important than the title.

We kiss. She starts undoing her own pants. I notice she's wearing two pair of thermal underwear, not one! … She had just gotten off an eight-hour shift. She hadn't been home in two days.

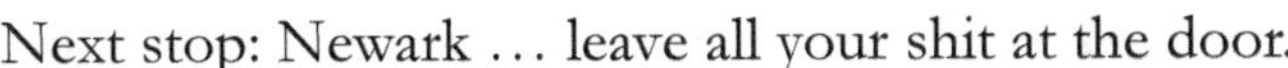

Next stop: Newark … leave all your shit at the door.

Mark's hand is out the window, tasting the universe, motioning for two bags. I'm poised to peal out, scanning the panorama, checking for cops and drive-by shenanigans … jazz is blasting down Broadway, down Martin Luther King Blvd … talking about it all … making plans.

Suckers! … all of them … and not the bag ladies. Not the dope fiend prostitutes. Not the stick-up artist growing in his trade: two days in, the crack-inspired insanity beginning to make sense … a modern cowboy! The black hat style … too down-and-out to contemplate a thing called "hip-hop" … second to second, ducking into allies. The endless mission: straight to the bottom.

It was the other ones … our parents … our schoolteachers … the whole establishment: Guilty! All of them … I myself now write this the accused. But at the time, we saw our escape:

Twenty thousand dollars … that's all we needed. I had about $2,000. But there's ways to make money.

I started out light: embezzlement … nothing new there, simply a change in venue. Instead of baseball hats and jerseys: $4,000 in body jewelry.

Mark's course was a little riskier: dropping out of school and all, devoting himself to the waitering circuit … a full-on, job-hopping party.

But whatever it takes: "$10,000 a piece in two years" … by that time I was due to graduate … we'd hop a plane back down to Costa Rica and buy some beachfront property. We had just gotten back; the surf was good, and the land was cheap. We had nightly meetings; broke out the map and red pens … you need to nourish a dream like that.

My family was getting nervous. Aside from Richie, my old crew couldn't really relate to me anymore, either … the long hair, perpetual shorts and sandals … bouncers stopped letting me into places I got into when I was 17.

"To be a writer," my dad would say, "you have to be somebody or know somebody" … so far, I have to admit, he's been right.

Even Mark was getting shaky. Somehow, someway, he had wrangled himself up $7,000 … he started with the subtle hints; that I had catching up to do.

The very next day I sold my Jeep … $13,000 in my pocket just like that. I had my share and airfare.

My old man didn't know what to say. There was some gibberish about his fruit-loop son moving out of America, about my proper schooling and even about the farm in Cuba. Somehow it had turned into a communist plot, my "moving back to a third-world country."

"But they're the only democracy in Central America, dad. And they don't even have an army … *we* back them."

Yeah, this type of thinking wasn't going over well with anyone really … I was becoming a royal pain in the ass.

"You and your pipe dreams" … that's Tracey. She had just graduated and moved back home to reality. All of a sudden: no more frat boys … my stock rose 300 percent.

When would the straight-laced, captain of the football team re-emerge? My dad, with his inside perspective, he wasn't accepting bets. There was no way to calculate that line.

I went underground, real deep. Barely noticed that I graduated. One day I was stoned reading Coleridge for three credits; the next I was reading Celine for the joy of it. Why walk down the isle?

Who would even come? Where would we go and what would we do afterwards?

Instead I went out and bought a machine, a shitty little Brother word processor that was too slow to keep up with me ... beeping, warning me to slow down ... When it finally caught up: a slew of red marks, misspellings ... green wavy lines all over the place!

———— ✻ ————

I need to make it clear that this is no phony baloney memoir, not like the Oprah-endorsed one by that writer with a toothache, a little noxious gas and an evening at the police station. I need to trust that you trust me. And if you don't, you can ... everything is absolutely verifiable! Accountable! ... Remember? I gave you fair warning: no way will you hear it all ... Impossible! Undesirable! ... but all verifiable! ... even the little unscheduled vacation at the Hackensack Medical Center's psychiatric ward.

How I got there? 100% disputable! Opinions will vary!

———— ✻ ————

I used to spend a lot of time drumming at The Wetlands ... you get inside your mind music ... tat, tat, tat ... booom ... tat, tat, tat ... booom. Then a claaack, claaack and back to the tat, tats.

There's a rhythm to it just like a river. Dependable if you know how to listen. Dependable but varying ... constant ... but bending and weaving through the ebbs and flows of pools, holes, rushes and falls. Inevitable infinite change but constant.

In the background a constant chack, chack, chack, chack ... chack, chack, chack, chack.

That's Vern with his homemade rattle. About 10- to 20 zils on a stick.

You learn to direct your mind, how to pick up on little nuances, alterations in sound. You learn how a change in yourself alters the rhythm of the stream.

If you're overly self-conscious or try too hard to take on the current, impose a tidal shift … your doomed. Toast. Destined for failure.

Vern could do it though.

He'd get that rattle shaking at remarkable speeds … hopelessly the drummers racing to keep up … chack, chack, chack, chack, chack, chack, chack, chack … Vern kept the rattle on infinite loop. Increasing in speed. Gushing … free-fall cascading all over us.

The dancers … arms shooting out here, legs there … hopping … jumping … twirling … the whole room in a frenzy… even the drunks against the walls bopping their heads. To be in The Wetlands basement was to be engulfed. A torrent of booming sound and smelly hippies.

You can't maintain a torrent … sooner or later the water pools. Deeper and deeper.

"Focus! Give me your quiet focus" … That's Vern. Urban Native American … old but how old? … faded silver ponytail … with a small metal-bawl marijuana pipe.

Again, he's asking for our focus. A quiet focus for "two brothers" arrested at a Rainbow Family Gathering. Apparently, these hippies were congregating in our National Forests, throwing week-long free parties where they fed everybody. He said anyone with a belly button was invited.

Naturally I checked it out … curiosity gets the best of me.

There's the drum circle … a constant vigil. At least 20 deep … the key is to pace yourself. The drums, the hippy chicks, the lunacy … the gibberish that comes out of these people's mouths. But it's working for them if sitting in a forest stoned with free meals is what they sought to accomplish.

There're hard drugs … don't let them fool you. Sketchy people doing sketchy things in tents … it's only natural. A sensual young crowd of drug takers … a sleepover party in the woods. Skinny dip showers in the afternoon pond.

Then out of nowhere: Doom! … more and more doom! … the doom compiles!

Rob Wondolowski plows into oncoming traffic … Jack Gilmore gets taken off life support within 48 hours.

The tragedies pile up … now it's my neighbors' turn … both the Gilmores and the Wondolowskis.

The sorrows.

The pains that get implanted into our lives.

The Gilmore's sorrows and the Wondolowski's pain intersecting within the neighborhood … separated by a few blocks and fences that we use to hop as kids.

My family?

Oh, we knew what everybody had in store … we got a three- or four-year head start on tragedy. We cleared the trail! We were making discoveries every day!

I realized I was interacting with the totality of reality. Actions, objects, thought and emotion intertwined. Internal and external … I call it God.

The songs on the radio were more accurate, more telling and guiding than any tarot card or I-Ching. Mind and intention like radio knobs … dial into your being.

Your mind is creating futures. The less clutter the more focus.

It's amazing what you can do.

Layers upon layers, depths of interlaced realities … a much larger world, a much larger and greater presence … you occupy the level at which you vibrate.

I had a professor who refused to concede that certain remarkable experiences or feelings were impossible to accurately convey with written words. I used to agree.

———— ∾ ————

Let me share the joy of being carried to bed, strapped down and injected with something to "calm you down." If you weren't mad going in, they'll help you adjust your perspective.

Initially, I was expecting a surprise party; that my whole family was already dialed into this higher plane of consciousness. But if they knew, why never a word? A little hint? Why all the problems?

No, it was a big mistake trying to explain myself. Turns out we weren't speaking the same language. Far from it.

My father and brother suggested we go for a ride. Why not? … only problem: it's been quite a day. A doozie to say the least … maybe just a little nap? In the back seat as we get underway? While we're still in familiar territory? … wake me up if you see something interesting.

… I trusted them.

… more importantly, I trusted God.

I peaked my head up as we turned into Hackensack Medical Center.

What's wrong?

Is Abuela O.K.?

The nurse taking my blood said her daughter liked the Grateful Dead.

… the white tiles on the walls, the metal gurneys … everything had a bright aura. There were reverberations left over from where I was. But I didn't go somewhere else. Somewhere else entered where I was.

I'm on an elevator with my good buddy nurse. We had a rapport.

I have to say, I was a little suspicious when the elevators opened to a medical unit. I was anticipating a late-night chat, a little intellectual jiu-jitsu with some third-rate psychologist who wasn't savvy enough to avoid the night shift.

Reality kicked in when they showed me to my room.

… absolutely zero intention of staying!

I bolt for the elevator but don't get many paces before I'm intercepted by a squad of orderlies. One grasping under each armpit and one right in my face.

I'm refusing pills so they're force feeding me like a reptile.

I take a play out of Bugs Bunny and fake a gulp, but they catch me. This only angers them … play time is over.

Now I'm up in the air. I'm crowd surfing … there's a bunch of big guys dressed in white below me.

I'm being held stiff as a board.

I notice the two-way mirror between the nurse station and the room they're carrying me into.

Here come the leather belt straps. They latch me down real good … I'm staying put if I like it or not.

And here comes the needle.

I should have taken the pills.

Night. Night. Like a good little boy.

⌁

There's a lady in the back of the cafeteria whining … she won't eat. It's something about the packaging and overall presentation. She's like that every meal.

What I don't understand is why they don't take her food out of the microwaveable tray … serve it to her on a plate like she's requesting.

It would save all our ears a lot of whining, sobbing, a wholesale of profanities.

There's a lot of kids … young teens … all bandaged up … wrists … necks … no explanations needed.

We get two, five-minute cigarette breaks a day … we all crowd the fire escape at once … if you're one of the unlucky ones who don't quite make it out, you lean over shoulders to sneak a peek at Hackensack's not-so-great outdoors. We're completely caged in. If there's a fire we'll all burn to death but nobody can jump.

There were a lot of group therapy sessions, circle jerks for folks who couldn't cope.

"I'm not crazy" … had to point that out right away … "My dad's just mad because I called the cops after he tried to kill himself. He wants to give me a taste of my own medicine." … "He thinks I'm nuts for wanting to move to Costa Rica." … "It doesn't even have its own army. Our military protects them."

Two days later my family shows up; it's great, a big reunion: My sister and her husband Julio … my brother … my dad … and could you believe it, they even had the good sense to bring Tracey … just so the whole fucking town would know.

I had to bum a quarter off my dad. I needed to call the head shop to explain my absence, but the orderlies took everything I had … my wallet, my belt. They were going to take my nose ring but I told them it was new and would close … they made an exception.

My father knew I was so mad he didn't even ask who I was going to call … it certainly wasn't going to be for weed … "Yeah, the 13th floor." … "Hackensack Medical Center."

I hung up the phone informed that I was fired.

The drive home the following Monday was the quietest and loneliest of my life … I was a refugee in the place of my birth. An outcast stranger amongst friends and family.

CHAPTER 8:

ON MY OWN

"A question that sometimes drives me hazy: am I or are the others crazy?"
— Albert Einstein

Condemned to be crazy … Fine! I fed into it:

"You know what Chris," I said to my brother, screaming up to him from the first floor. "I'm going to make it rain tomorrow just to prove it to you. Not because I think I can, or because I believe I can … I know I can!"

Can you believe it fucking rained?

I wasn't shocked … I was shocked that I woke to a perfectly sunny day. Not a hint of a cloud … blue everywhere!

"How the hell is it going to rain like this," I thought to myself … a real fucking noodle.

I was expecting grey, no airplanes … hear 'em overhead, setting up to land at Newark International, sure, but don't count on seeing one.

Forget it! You could see them a mile up in the sky … trailing long streaks of aluminum. Barium. They're spraying us real good.

My dad said they were B-52 bombers when I asked as a kid … "The trail dad? The trail?" I was dying to know… even at that age a pain in the ass.

"How can you say that's a B-52 and not a 747?" …. "It's a mile up!" … "A faint metallic blip!"

But that's not important. What's important is that it rained … and that I knew it would. Didn't matter if the clouds gathered late afternoon, if it was merely the dropping of the Summer day's accumulated moisture … "Close the windows!" … You should've heard the drops smashing against the aluminum siding … heavy sheets of water cascading off the roof … and then gone … stillness.

I had $13,000 but it was meaningless. It disgusted me. Each bill a portion of a Costa Rican bamboo surf shack that wouldn't be erected … the aroma of tropical surf wax and low-tide reef was fading fast. Mark was weary of me. Costa Rica became out of the question … I might as well've torched the whole fucking pile of money. "Up in smoke." Yeah, Cheech & Chong … I wasn't laughing. I wasn't quite sure of who I was anymore … No football captain. No black belt karateka. No fucking mother. Would any of this have happened if she was around? I knew better than to ask … pointless.

Destiny is destiny, so all I could do was direct it. But I had nowhere I wanted to go; nowhere that I should be proud to admit to anyway. I wanted to go crazy! I wanted to escape into the streets! Into the night! Anywhere! Give me more life! … I wanted to jot it all down and did.

In my mind, I was a big shot author already … I was really cracking up. You should've seen these sentences … juvenile … low level. It had soul, but the publishers and agents — the ones I randomly called on, buzzed up to their offices from the lobby — they weren't impressed. Hell, I'm lucky they didn't call the cops. A delinquent with a manila folder.

I Shanghaied their ass at *Relix Magazine*. Walked right into the heart of their editorial department ... blank stares all around. I might as well of had the publisher's head in my hands.

"Can we help you?"

A longhaired white boy in Brooklyn, fresh off two trains and a bus ... damn straight I needed some help. And why was the pizza so bad? The corner pizzeria: a New York disgrace. You call this Brooklyn? I was looking for *Do the Right Thing* ... authentic Italian, racial tension. Instead: two Iraqis.

"I'm looking for Tony Brown." I said it with a confidence that suggested not only that I was an acquaintance, but that I could identify her by a freckle on her ass. Which would have been convenient, because she was sitting four feet away with her back to me. The truth was out: I was a weirdo subscriber that got the publisher's name off the masthead ... Who's subscribing? I stole my *Relix* from work. The two-bit head shop that wouldn't have me back.

"I have a manuscript that I thought you might be interested in."

Some balding, past his prime middle-aged hippie chose to intercede on behalf of his colleagues ... wouldn't you know it, he asked *the* question: "What's it about?"

What's it about? I just spent 720 hours banging this thing out. Shall I share its meaning with you in 30 seconds, sum it up in one precisely calculated sentence that I memorized? Maybe I should. Maybe someone will buy my books.

So now I'm back underground, doing the things that I do: surfing, drumming, wondering the streets by bike or skateboard ... no hour off limits, no neighborhood too sketchy.

There was a certain song to the streets that played me, the instrument.

The hookers on Broad St. ... the lowest ... find me a more down-trodden ... black men blending into the urban environment. Hoods up, heads down ... brick-front tenements, chain-linked fences cordoning off corner liquor stores ... Be careful! Watch your eyes; watch your swagger! Not too much! ... just enough. Don't seem too glad ... not here ... total blasphemy.

CHAPTER 9:

EVEN THE SEAGULLS OVERHEAD

"… and then you realize that your experience and relationship with God supersedes all the scriptures, all the dogmas and claims. A Unique Testament!"—Me. I said that.

I watched her dance for weeks mesmerized by her bouncing around. A little petite blonde dreadlocked dervish twirling, skipping, hopping to the Grateful Dead.

… backless patchwork tank tops.

… silver bells anklet.

… the thick blue Venetian glass bead braded on her backpack with hemp.

I couldn't take it anymore. I came right out with it one night, tapping her on the shoulder; interrupting her internal conversation: "You're beautiful."

She just said "thanks," backed away enough to continue her musical salutation and faded into a sea of undulating hippies.

I thought about her constantly after that, sensing that I would see her at the Wetlands and then doing so … or not, and wondering where she was and what she was doing. I heard she was from Long Island. I pictured her living in a large house on a deserted windswept beach, dunes pushing their way ever closer. I envisioned her father a doctor or lawyer, maybe a stockbroker or so rich that he could afford to be nothing at all … I had heard about these Long Island hippie types; the Jewish trust fund babies.

I decided to take a drive; tied the boards to the roof of my jalopy and headed over the George Washington Bridge … waaaay out of place passing through the Bronx … I had no idea … avoid all signs for Upstate! I knew that much … Long Island! Long Island! … I had my eye on the prize. I thought it was a small community. That if I drove around I'd find her soon enough.

"Sunrise Hwy."

Seemed like a better exit than most, particularly with my thermostat hopping around in the red zone … a delicate balancing act of open windows, blasting the heat and prayer.

"Long Beach."

… another good sign … let's just hope not *too* long … the needle's already taking a nap below the waist of the "H." … the engine's smoking. There's the familiar smell of boiling coolant.

Don't touch the radiator cap! I know it's tempting.

Pull over! Read a book! Let it cool on it's own. You have no idea how many times I've seen the neon-green waterfall. A Niagara Falls of coolant. Whirlpools of toxin forming under the car … stay back! When it's done crackling and hissing … that's when you tend to things … pour water in, add oil or piss on it … whatever it takes … you can get it home! … unless you can't.

I hit the end of the road: a spray-painted cinderblock graffiti mural holding up the boardwalk … where were the mansions? Except for the beach it looked like home.

Could I surf here? Was it clean? Better lock the doors from the looks of it.

I booked up the boardwalk. There wasn't a lot of light left … 2- to 3 feet and crappy! It looked cold too. Early-April grey: the water, the sky and the fog.

I put the wetsuit on anyway … the boots, the gloves, the hood. I wax up and jump in. There're two or three other guys out. We're all desperate; making the most of the mush.

There she is! It's her. I can feel her standing against the boardwalk rail looking out to sea …. and there she is again jogging … and on roller blades … and a bike … and then she was all of them and even the seagulls overhead.

It's Tuesday and I know the Zen Tricksters or the Juggling Suns or Lost Marbles or any number of tripped-out Grateful Dead cover bands will be playing at The Wetlands … and Rainbow Family will be there too, and I'll find myself in the middle of a drum circle leading the whole thing, or being led against my knowledge and I'll dance, hair down to cover the shame I still felt … something, somewhere still didn't want to cross over, was too aware of itself or not aware at all of who or what I could become … Still with me? I'm not sure I am but that's how these nights go sometimes.

No school. No work … No surf either. I go ride my skateboard; turn everything into waves anyway.

Curbs.

… pathetic ankle biters.

Cars.

… getting much better. Chest high zippers pealing down the block.

Trucks and tall bushes.

… Grab your balls bro! Now it's waaaaay overhead!!!

I wound up at the Montclair Bookstore and started wandering … past the Kerouac, past the Celine, Bukowski and Burroughs, past all these great writers that are literary movements unto themselves.

Now I'm sitting in the children's section, totally amused by Doctor Seuss' *Daisy-Head Mayzie* … the girl with the flower growing out of her head! You know she's going to cut it off; because of the ridicule, the subjugation … I thought of Amie and how the last time I saw her at the Wetlands her dreadlocks were gone.

Did daddy make her cut them? Did she graduate law school and finally give in? Conform?

Later that night I threw that kid's book in my backpack along with a water bottle, notebook, tobacco tin holding five joints and a Grateful Dead Rasta teddy bear … the later was something I snagged from the head shop before they fired me. Lava lamps, black lights, multiple incense burners … I wanted to give them all away now. Reverse the karma.

I jumped on the Gary Fischer mountain bike my sister left behind. The one Julio scored "off the back of a truck." My family knew more gangsters and crooked politicians than doctors and lawyers … we didn't know any doctors or lawyers.

I snap off a sunflower from the neighbor's mini-lawn on the corner. Had to do it then. It would only get more ghetto as I got closer to the PATH train. Find me a tree! Well, maybe in the park. But better stick to the lighted road and don't dillydally … you better be swift on that bike. Remain a moving target.

I hopped on the PATH, bike and all, settling down to scribble in my notebook. On a Tuesday night, heading into the city, the train's kind of empty. But not completely … colorful companions: young, old, black, white. But not all-American white. Very few of those. Mostly Italians and Hispanics. Second generation at best. Asians, Arabs, Hindus.

Once in the city I biked past NYU, Washington Square Park and Gray's Papaya ... where Richie and I saw the dead guy gasping for air. He wasn't dead yet. But with a few bullet holes in his chest it didn't look promising ... past the Haitians selling incense from sidewalk folding tables. Past the used booksellers and Village freaks. Past Houston ... jutting off to the West Side onto cobblestone streets. Dilapidated high rises and delinquent factories ... they're missing their smokestacks. Yet the trucks still come and go. And here and there an upscale club ... patrons dressed like they're going to the prom.

I roll up to The Wetlands in my surf trunks. I chain the bike to the lamppost ... a heavy lock ... a heavier chain. Careful to wind it through the frame and both tires. I take the seat post with me.

First stop: the bathroom ... to run some cool water over my wrists; splash a little on my face. But before I could get there, I'm intercepted by a radiant being on the stairwell; her presence momentarily stopping time.

"Oh, I, uh, thought you were somebody else," I said, trying to excuse my gaze.

"Maybe I am who you though I was," she replied ... And she was right!

The Rasta Bear and sunflowers broke the ice and got her attention, but when I pulled out the *Daisy-Head Mayzie* ... boy did that work in my favor.

I got her number. Plans were made. We decided Long Beach would be great neutral territory.

Getting there would be another story!

It was just before the George Washington Bridge when I started smoking (the car, not me); I had 30 yards to fight my way to the shoulder before hitting the tollbooths … those E-Z Pass bastards weren't giving me an inch, not easing up at all.

I make the shoulder, traverse a couple orange cones and pop the hood … a reverse Niagara Falls! … steam, water, coolant … everything billowing up in the air … a toxic sauna right under my nose.

Hmm … let me guess. What to do? … Uh, how about nothing?

Even if I could see the tubing and metallic mess through the smoking abyss I wouldn't know what to do with them … I stood around the front of the car simply for ornamental sake, for protocol. I wasn't worried … rudimentary situation! Just let it cool down. Remember? Water. Oil … Jalopy 101.

I was back on the road before I knew it, inching along confronted by road signs and bumper-to-bumper traffic … long reflective green banners overhead: BQE, Cross Island Pkwy, Long Island Expressway … arrows shooting off in all directions … underpasses, overpasses, and out my passenger-side window: Manhattan.

The Southern State was a barren dessert, except instead of sand: cars … humble little two door, hatch-back foreign jobs; huge SUVs and a shit ton of Mercedes and BMWs … you would've though they were giving them away.

Me? Unemployed … Unemployable!!!! My car spewing smoke from the corner of its lip.

Over to the side of the road again! This time it's a doozey. I could see what the problem was right away because the smokestack was centralized, a real Old Faithful jetting from a gash in the radiator hose … this was going to take a certain level of ingenuity.

I found a ball of tinfoil on the side of the road, unfolded it and broke out the duct tape … once, twice, three … four … five times around … "That should hold."

And it did … about five more miles up the road … and then it was over to the shoulder again. I didn't even look. I felt it die; dispense all of its vital fluids with one last shuttering clunk.

"OK. Fuck the car. I just need to get to the beach."

No sooner did I think this than a mighty pickup truck pulls in behind me; the kind with an extra set of rear wheels, an exterior chrome-plated toolbox and a winch.

A cowboy-hat-wearing man gets out, says hello and starts attaching my car to his rear fender. I try explaining that I don't have any money but now he's busy placing my boards in the back of his truck.

"So, where you heading," he asked.

"Long Beach," I said.

"That's not so close. You need a ride?"

"Yeah. But are you going that way?"

"Sort of."

We left it at that.

With neither Amie nor I working, my $13,000 … it was like a NASA shuttle launch. We were counting down.

For a little skinny hippy chick, a vegetarian … boxes and boxes, cartons of pizza rolls!

Good thing she could still eat cheese!

… and fish!

… and lobster!

A non-observant vegetarian Jew.

Her divorced mother wasn't working, either. Temporary medical leave … Fibromyalgia … any given moment, out of the blue … excruciating pain! Got to pop pills and get to bed. For hours. For days.

Amie wanted to see Phish in Maine, "The Great Went" at Loring Air Force Base … so we went.

Non-stop traffic to the first rest area in Connecticut … it's like a Dead show ... Frisbees. Hacky Sacks. Devils Sticks.

I strike up a conversation with some kids who tell me they're "from earth" and "just roaming around" while I wait for Amie to bring back the Taco Bell. Our righteous, meatless 7-Layer Burritos, Cinnamon Twists and gargantuan sodas.

Good thing we're being health conscious.

I watch our little roaming earthlings drive off in their parent's $80,000 Land Rover; chopsticks in hand as they clumsily plucked at their sushi.

I was growing bitter. It was over for me before it even started … definitely the wrong side of the tracks. South of Midland Ave.

The vibe was heavy at The Wetlands; you walked right smack-dab into it crossing the threshold. It was like that some nights … the intensity.

Low lighting. Flashing strobes. Multi-colored spotlights … And sound! A reverberating atmosphere enhanced by pungent smoke.

There goes Dave, DJ Gravy sneaking off backstage with bricks in his backpack: Sour Diesel Bud. $550 an ounce.

As usual, I have to pardon myself. A little freshening up in the loo. It's my way. Especially on these nights. Run a little water over the wrists. A splash to the face.

There's Vern.

He's agitated.

I've never seen him agitated.

He's pacing … not too far … the bathroom's not that big. Three heavily graffitied stalls.

He's hitting a small brass pipe while running laps … like a little Choo-Choo blowing smoke. Tight concentric circles behind me while I'm finishing up with the once over in the sink. Giving the forearms a good soaking.

Now I'm ready to chitchat. Now I could be of some assistance.

A friend?

A dire friend in need, he says.

A hand-written manuscript needs editing *and* retyping … immediately!

Immediately?

Immediately! Right now!

Well, maybe not right now. Not with Dave and the band about to go on upstairs.

I pocket the number. Good thing Amie's mom bought her that computer … no longer an amenity. I foresee some typie typie in my future.

The best thing I have going for me walking down 7th Ave. is that this guy doesn't know me. Not a clue.

I'm wearing a tie. It's like my college days … people respect people who wear ties.

I'm wearing a jacket, too. I got all dolled up for this guy.

It's right off 7th Avenue in Chelsea. The neighborhood doesn't look like much, very commercial, but everyone's dressed real well.

Up elevator!

… I don't like it. I don't trust it. It's old and originally intended to move freight eons ago.

The only thing this elevator has going for it is the petite brunette in the corner. She's a model … or at least I think she's a model … she could be a model and they say models live around here. Either that or her parents are sporting her rent and N.Y.U.

I get off a few floors up and there he is, the author. A strange little man in his late 50s. He's got one heck of an accent. It's too thick to fight through. I can't pinpoint it … plus he's walking away from me.

It's a huge open space. Industrial. Long rows of workbenches. Nondescript hardware scattered about. Metal cabinets. Multi-tiered trays with wheels … the place could use a sweeping. A good once over with Glass Plus.

He hands me a manila folder and five $100 bills … there's the promise of five more $100 bills and another manila folder, weekly, as long as I keep bringing them back typed and on disc.

We set up a nice little barter system. I struggle with his chicken scratch and he pays me extremely well.

His main character is a lovable but goofy Nazi private. A good-hearted buffoon who struggles with protocol and maintaining focus … it's not easy … his penmanship. It's as thick as his accent. And there're all these cross outs and little notes in the margins with squiggly arrows pointing everywhere but the whole thing is written in pencil. Smeared pencil. This guy drags his writing hand. That's undeniable.

A month later I'm in a rented tuxedo for a Jewish wedding in Midtown. One of Amie's friends … everyone has so much more money than me.

It doesn't take a lot.

But this worry … this concern of having to make payments. For rent. To put food in my mouth … there is no vacation from it. Not for me.

I buy my moments when I get a chance … $400 an ounce … I get the "I know Dave discount" because I know Hugo.

I step outside … stepping outside from this gig, though, is a doozy. It's waaaay outside.

Down elevator!

This is the way to do it … black marble with gold trim! Mirrors! Shiny!

Obviously, I get some ideas. Fantasies … there's lots of hot young Jewish girls upstairs. Their lame boyfriends are too busy trying to one up each other to squeeze their asses.

I'd squeeze their asses but I'm down here on the corner with my St. Peter's College English degree … and a joint. A fat one! … If I'm going to buy my moments I'm going to relish them.

I got a good vantage point from here. It's late, these Jews know how to throw a good party … I can see up and down both sides of the empty street and the elevator doors are set a good way back. I can see anyone coming from any direction.

And who should I see strolling down the street at 1:00 a.m?

… fucking Vern!

It's always now you see me now you don't with this guy. But here he is. In the flesh.

He tells me about his buddy. Two Can Sam with his Fruit Loop chicken scratch.

German scientist! Engineer! Supplies parts to NASA!

That threw me for a loop.

Well, Vern's got to go … he's on his way … *puff puff* and pass on by. Toodaloo.

A few weeks go by. Vern's little Project Paperclip amateur author has me rolling in dough. I can hardly keep up with him. He's pushing these manila folders down my throat.

I'm a little jealous. This fucker's going to get published before me … I got the best marketing plan … keep everything in my drawer! … no website! … no blog!

I learned what they do to you when you open your mouth. Just a little peep. A slight but genuine gesture.

CHAPTER 10:

SELLING OUT TO POVERTY

"I read somewhere that 77 percent of all the mentally ill live in poverty. Actually, I'm more intrigued by the 23 percent who are apparently doing quite well for themselves." — Jerry Garcia.

A man gets so lonely sometimes, so tired. Even now, the words … like lead fingers over the keyboard. Not the worked all day "I'm pooped" tired. But the "I've been working so long and don't see no end to it" exhausted … the kind that keeps you on the couch.

415 West Broadway, Long Beach, N.Y, 11561 … directly across the street from the boardwalk, right there on the corner. If you look just right, on a good swell, you could see the waves. In fact, after my first night's sleep in the place it was going off: 6 foot and perfect! Like a dream … wish I could say the same about the pad.

The whole apartment … kitchen, bathroom, parlor, bedroom … all one room … like a lazy Transformer, all things at once. The futon set the mood; either folded up for company or sprawled out to sleep … night, night. Sometimes even I got confused.

82

It was usually after dinner, when I was getting comfortable and settling down, that Amie's friends would show up ... to smoke my weed. And then talk amongst themselves about what a downer I was.

The fuck they would know ... with one or two beaded dreadlocks in their head, fashionable patchwork outfits and matching shoes ... new, different shoes every time I see them. Perpetually "going to school" ... in and out of majors ... to Binghamton ... to N.Y.U. ... to Cornell ... anywhere but to work!

The $13,000 from selling my Jeep? ... kaput ... insto presto ... down to $1,500 and rent was due. Forget the old $256.62. That's child's play! Now we're at $750 a month ... and that was after first month rent, last month rent, security and realtor fee.

I was still trying to be a writer, too, though I lacked my own typing machine. What I happened to hold onto were some foolish ideals about not degrading myself in some Manhattan office. So instead I took a shady job with a Jewish Mafioso the next town over.

The outfit was familiar. I've seen it a thousand times:

A mid-sized warehouse on some dead-end industrial road, very non-assuming. They started me off very college-grad-like ... on a computer. I knew Microsoft Word. Unfortunately, they wanted me to shine in Excel ... a bunch of tiny boxes, graphs. I faked it for as long as I could. I asked a lot of rudimentary questions. The office geek, the manager, the one who had a heart attack from a late-night coke binge, he was a wizard. He could do it all on a PC and expected me to follow suit.

A truck would back in and drop off a hundred boxes of Nike jackets or Fila shoes or any number of branded products ... mostly clothes. A gang of five, consisting of one Irish special forces Vietnam vet; an old black man, also one-time army but seeing no action so always regarded as a tier or two below the expert; his crack selling son; and a young Puerto Rican kid with a lot of energy to fuck around but never to do anything productive ... these four loaded and unloaded trucks while a washed-up guy from Long Beach with a beer belly and tight sweat pants supervised. He never got his hands dirty.

In and out the trucks would go, at least three, four times a day. I felt like a heel dressed in a buttoned-down shirt at the desk; like a traitor.

Big Boss Man Arty sat in the back office with the door open smoking cigars, talking on the phone about upcoming fights in Vegas. Of course, he'll be ringside … his office walls were adorned with framed autographed photos of celebrity fighters, ball players, actors and politicians. He was only missing the Pope.

So, there I go, checking shipments and matching contents with bills of laden … never even heard that phrase before. It wasn't something we covered in school.

The trucks back in. The warehouse guys unload the boxes and stack them into little neat rows … the items come out of one box and right back into another … a little switcheroo … new hangers … new labels. Many times the stuff goes out on the same truck it came in on. It was done very efficiently, or could have been, if not for the knuckleheads.

Arty, the wannabe-Italian Jew, he's obviously in a no-blabber-mouth business. He's dealing with people that know how to keep their trap shut… *"Psst"*…. "I got some phony baloney Chinese Nikes" … "85 percent off."

My office supervisor played with his computer a lot. If not out-right video games, learning some new program for some future job he intended to get. He had grown up with Arty and there was certainly some pity involved. He was surviving off Arty's scraps. We all were.

<div style="text-align:center">~~~</div>

Things got busy around Christmas. It was like a truck stop on the New Jersey Turnpike at that place; trucks coming and going. That two-bit crew couldn't keep up … With tensions mounting and my computer incompetence starting to reveal itself, I did what I've been trained to do … I offered to help unload a truck.

Of course, the very next day, before I could even sit down and turn on my monitor: "Ray, can you help them out in the warehouse?"

I got the hint. No one had to tell me. You can say I stopped wearing collared shirts.

Loading, unloading. Packing, repacking. Taping up boxes and piling them up in the corner nice and neat, waiting for a truck to come. I became an expert with a hand truck, a luxury we didn't have at UPS. At UPS, if you wanted a box somewhere, you better bend the fuck over and pick it up.

The guys in the warehouse were great, they always are. The army guys thought I was a fool for not signing up … free room and board they said, plus see the world. Sounded good, but what about the morning runs? That was my concern. Special Forces said Vietnam was the party of a lifetime; but I got a sense it was more of a party than he bargained for … you could smell the hard stuff on his breath first thing in the morning.

At lunch we'd all break and pull out our sandwiches, bitch about the management … I wondered if they had anything to say about me before I joined their ranks. Now I was part of the crew. Hell, I worked five times harder than any of them. How do you watch an old man struggle with a box from across the room?

"Special Forces, what ya doing? Why don't you just stay up there and pick?"

It's always easier to toss the boxes down from up in the truck than having to cart them across the warehouse, stack them, then come back and do the same thing again and again for eight hours. Either way it's eight hours of lifting, but gravity can be your untrustworthy friend. Helping you now, smashing a toe later.

The holidays passed and the trucks slowed to a trickle. They let Special Forces go, saying he called out sick one time too many, but we knew it was the pinch of the slowdown. Why didn't they let him go in mid-December when he was noticeably drunk? Or when he got into it with the warehouse supervisor and just walked off? … because we needed him then the same way the government did in '67 … all the hands we could get. And for practically nothing. How these guys fed themselves, let alone their families, was a mystery to me.

The Puerto Rican kid just stopped coming one day; he must have found a better gig to goof off at.

Me? I stopped working in the office weeks ago but was praying to retain my paid services as a human mule … college fucking degree? … 3.75 grade point average? … shivering in snow up to my ankles! "Come on. Pile another box on, its fucking freezing out here."

My degree didn't matter; my time came just like everyone else's. I could smell the freshly sharpened ax blade as I got called into the office.

～

Goddamn. I felt like I got kicked in the teeth. And telling Amie was no picnic either … we were barely getting by as it was.

We worried. We argued. We bickered back and forth. We did everything possible in fits of passion except fuck.

I called my sister. She told me I could move in with her and Julio if worse came to worst … it appeared I was standing in the center of that intersection.

To add insult to injury there was a message on the machine. *Relix Magazine* wanted me to come and pick up my manuscript. Tony Brown, the onetime publisher, had moved on … my words were getting stale and they didn't want to waste the postage sending it back.

I had no job, the book I was counting on to save me was dead and rent was due in two weeks … we were already down to Ramen Noodles and cereal; and Amie's cereal was a little too extravagant for the budget.

Of course, Amie was all smiles with the $13,000 … breakfasts, lunches, dinners … trips all over the place … into the city … all the clubs. Now, trapped in this tiny apartment, she was getting antsy. She didn't really care about the bare foot strolls across the street with the surfboard. She didn't really care about me… it was time to abandon ship.

"Ray, we can't live like this," she would say.

"Like what," I'd say, getting defensive. "How many college students you know get to live on the beach? Without paying rent?"

This type of logic, while true, only pissed her off. She hated that I "threw the money in her face" … though she never tried to dodge it. In fact, she let it hit her right dab in the center of her bulbous forehead.

I stormed up the boardwalk feeling like a loser. When a man can't do what a man is supposed to do — in the eyes of women, other men, his father — he can't escape far enough.

My feet rested on the boardwalk bench where my ass should've been and my ass balanced on the backrest. It was a cold but clear night, beautiful … stars twinkled across the horizon and a small dark wave broke on the shoreline, barely visible. Its existence betrayed by a thin sliver of collapsing crest.

No doubt my sister called my dad as soon as I put down the phone. I could count on that. They were all worried about me but I knew my father … he wouldn't have me back and I wouldn't go.

I'd be forced to figure something out while staying with my sister. Save a couple bucks and just disappear. Do it how I dreamt: Broke and all alone in a Newark tenement right beside McCarter HWY …

just a typewriter and a shattered soul. What a life it turned out to be … kicked in the balls at every turn.

"God, what's going on?" I demanded to know!

"What happened? … I listened! I trusted! I believed!"

The stars just kept twinkling. The waves lapping the shoreline.

With that I walked the saddest walk of my life … down the boardwalk ramp back to my tiny apartment, each step further from redemption.

I climbed the flight of stairs, opened the door and threw my jacket across the back of the unit's lone chair … it blew a handwritten note off the table:

Amie loved me … she was heart broken … she had gone for a bike ride.

She was a good one, she just couldn't understand … what I had been through, where I had come from and, most of all, that I looked towards her to bring some light back into my life.

Speaking of light, the fucking red dot on the answering machine was going crazy.

"Great," I thought. "My dad."

Begrudgingly he's going to offer me the basement for a bit. And I'd have to take it. I'd rather inconvenience him than my newlywed sister … I figured when push came to shove — even after feeding my ass and putting me through private school — he owed me. He wouldn't let me sink … would he?

I hit the button to stop the blinking … the way the day was going I wanted to take it straight between the eyes, get it all out and over with.

"Amie Laino, this is Abe from Abe's Pitaria," said an unfamiliar voice. "I kept your name and number on file, but I could really use somebody right away. Call me back."

It was too late to call anyone, but my spirit was immediately uplifted and I felt ashamed for questioning my circumstances.

In my darkest hour…

CHAPTER 11:

FABULOUS DISHWASHER

"Faith is taking the first step even when you don't see the whole staircase." —
Martin Luther King, Jr.

So lets take inventory: New haircut but no money; new monthly payments but no car.

What I did have was a drippy sink … a rusty bathroom radiator … everything so on top of each other you have to sit sidesaddle on the throne … very conducive, let me tell you.

6:00 a.m. and I'm on my skateboard. How's that for four wheels? … forget vroom, vroom, vroom … Running late? … push, push, push! from here to eternity! … I'm not a little kid anymore … twenty-five years old, college degree. Time to show some responsibility, to make a move … I was movin' alright: 9 miles an hour.

Elbow deep in suds at the back basin, being careful not to palm a knife as I feel around for utensils … I get the hunch bathing an open wound in this mess wouldn't be good.

Strange how an establishment looks so different from the back … looking over the counter at you, the customer. You have such faith in these hands … in me and this illegal immigrant from El Salvador. He obviously has experience cutting tomatoes. You don't waste that sort of talent in the sink.

Abe, the owner, really tried to be a nice guy. He talked music and painting and even weed with me; he'd tell me about the customers and which one of his wife's friends he wanted to fuck. But the truth of the matter is, he couldn't handle the crowds.

More than two people in the store? The phone ringing? Look out!!! … cooking gyro ain't for the squeamish.

His father ran the joint on Sundays … I'd never known a real asshole before. Everyone has their first … he had something to say about everything. A real expert … he tuned me to the fact that I'd been tying my shoes incorrectly all this time. He chewed me out for mistakenly writing "Beach St." on a delivery ticket when it should have read "Beech."

"You're going to have him driving in circles. He's going to be out for an hour" … That's him red faced. If he ain't careful he's going to keel over into the orzo salad, but he keeps going. "There isn't even a Beach Street in this god damn city."

How should I know?

All the sand!

The seagulls!

… those weren't rose bushes I smelled every morning at low tide, were they?

"Well, if there isn't a Beach St., then I'm sure he knows what it means." That's me covering my tracks. Using a little finesse.

Sure as shit, Manny, the delivery guy, he's back in five minutes … makes no mention of the mix up. And he's a literate fucker too, another college-grad genius … multiple degrees in computer programming … we're the best educated gyro and falafel staff in the world.

Joe Veroba. Now there's a good friend. Right up the block ... bong hit after bong hit ... gurgle, gurgle, gurgle.

Never harsh! You'll do more than you should, more than you can handle ... you'll be excusing yourself.

Don't worry. Little walks ... to the kitchen, to the bathroom. Up the block to check the surf.

He had his own garden. Very secretive!!! Only half the block knew ... me being the new neighbor and all, he'd fill me in. Not right away though, I had to earn my stripes.

"Damn Joe, it always smells so good in here."

"Oh, it's the air fresheners," he said, looking away and disappearing into the other room. He had a Taj Mahal ... separate kitchen, bath and chilling sleep space.

Air fresheners? I had to take a look! Amie kept a clean house but this was ridiculous.

"No, it's not this" ... that's me with my nose an inch away from the plug-in Febreze. "Something smells fruity in here."

"Rack 'em." ... that's Joe from the other room. Always interrupting; changing the subject to bong hits ... I hear the bong stop bubbling. His gurgle had dissipated ... there's the long exhale ... and now *he* wants to check the surf.

We both know it will be flat ... I had just gotten back from my little stroll, my little "I got to get some air."

Sure enough: flat ... beautiful summer day. Cars everywhere. Girls on rollerblades. Guys on rollerblades! Never a pretty sight ... Joe's hopping away on his skateboard. It's time to be alone. I see him grinding 360s ... all the way around ... like the hand on the watch I did not own.

God gave us all the seed-bearing plants to use, right? Says so right there in the Bible, doesn't it?

Granted, Joe's plants were cloned. If you found a seed, at $500 an ounce, you held on to it. Johnny Appleseed didn't have shit on Joey V.

His mini forest of clones was ready to go and as far as we could tell Amie's mom was copasetic to our needs; her backyard was perfect: it had dirt.

Amie had tried her hand at this sort of thing once before but with mixed results: the plants grew tall but produced no buds. That's from her own mouth … OK, we wouldn't be taking her advice … a silent partner all the way. But we would be needing her Jeep.

It wasn't a long ride, 15 miles at most — eight or nine of them on the quiet south end of the Meadowbrook Highway ... I knew where the cops liked to hide. Still, we had over a half dozen clones in the back. We were a little stinky.

Amie and Joe kept assuring me how lax the New York laws were, but I'd heard about guys staying overnight for possessing a joint, for getting caught puffing a bowl on the subway platform … it was obvious we weren't transporting Christmas trees.

We arrived without incident, though our vehicle could've been a little less conspicuous … with Joe having to spark up … the Grateful Dead, Bob Marley and surf sticker detailing. The little smoke signals floating out the back.

It was now time to dig some holes.

Joe was very specific about it: two feet by two feet by two feet.

"Exact?"

"Exact!"

Apparently, he was going to watch to make sure I did it right. I had to carry in the fertilizer, too. When you're big, everyone thinks you're fucking Hercules.

It's not a complicated operation.

Stick the plants in the ground, fill it in until there's a slight mound; pat it all down lightly — that's it. Thirty minutes tops. The summer's sun and Amie's mom would do the rest. If she wanted to go crazy with the hose so be it ... but not too much! Again, Joe's personal instructions. I wanted to tell him that he was going overboard, that they're very resilient plants. But then again, he knew what he was doing. His methods were tried and true.

Time for a surf.

Time to send out a few resumes ... can't flip pita my whole life.

Time to take some bad acid.

Time to sit on the floor while Amie's friends hog the futon: Jed, Flammer, super keyboardist George ... they all have a crush on her. Brian Faulkner, too ... I'm about to checkmate him at the Chess Forum when he tells me her mom walked in on them once.

September came and went ... I wasn't the happiest guy in town. Far from it ... Instead of a love nest, a fucking Ramada Inn! Nassau County hippies all over the place, bunking on my floor ... guys in beards, chunky girls with armpit hair. But what can you expect after a harvest?

Joe, in all of his modesty, he was predicting four- to five ounces apiece. This after some hardcore botany he pulled out when things got crucial, when the plants started playing peak-a-boo over the neighbor's fence ... I freaked out. I admit it ... I didn't want Amie or her mother to panic and pull the plants — not with those ba-nana-sized buds — but I didn't want them to lose the house, either.

Joe, as nonchalant as could be, he bends the plants in two. He folds them in half and stakes the tippy tops into the ground … so much for the baby treatment.

"You know how the top cone is always the biggest? Well, this whole thing is going to be like that," he said to me, waving his hand along the inverted U of the trunk.

We didn't get four- to five ounces … we got 33! … Our freezer was full of mason jars … every cubbyhole in our tiny apartment was stuffed tight with weed. Even with the incessant mooching we couldn't make a dent.

Doug up the block, he couldn't understand why we wouldn't sell him an ounce for $200.

"Ray, you got it for nothing." He kept on with the guilt trip like a broken record.

"Dude, I'll smoke you out for free all day. But I can't just give an ounce away. When all this buds gone, I'm going to be paying $500 an ounce, too … I'll give it to you for $400."

Things were going my way. To top it off, my resume got through. The local paper invited me in for an interview.

Luckily for me, the executive editor happened to be a little portly and desperate … she was giving me the eye. What was experience amongst new friends? The five what?

I showed her a few poems, ones without drugs or sex.

"Not bad. You can write. I'll have to spend some time teaching you the AP style but when can you start?"

It was then I saw it all unfold; while still sitting in the interview chair:

Bombarded at the pitaria on a Friday night! … Walk ins, folks calling left and right … calling back to change an order at the last minute … "But it went out already. It will be at least another 45 minutes."

They still want it! They're willing to pay for both orders if they have to.

Bossman was about to blow his top; I could feel it.

… I was overjoyed. My moment was coming. Mark had told me about it many times.

Like clockwork: Bossman's hands in the air! the huffing! the puffing! multiple superlatives! … In front of everybody! No shame. Double cracking the whip … I disappear into the back. I know what he's thinking: "This dimwit has screwed up the order of his chores again! He should be doing jumping jacks up here with me. Not back there washing a plate or two."

I throw my hooded sweatshirt on, grab my skateboard and hightail it past the Friday-night crowd. Everyone's aware of what's happening.

"Just like that, you're leaving me here like this?" … Now Abe wants to be buddies for real. He throws me a disheartened look. He's disappointed. Worse, he's desperate. He's in need. He's sinking fast.

I was on a plane to Puerto Rico a few days later. Amie and I were going to catch some waves and when we got back I'd start a new job, a new career. We didn't know we were doomed. You never do.

CHAPTER 12:

JOURNALISTIC JESTER

"I have a theory that the truth is never told during nine-to-five hours." — *Hunter S. Thompson.*

Hold on a second! I know the temptation!

"See! This is where he gets his break!"

I was whining like that when I read Jack Kerouac got assigned to his local paper, the Lowell Sun ... it always looks easy for the other guy.

Two weeks of work? Two weeks of getting up and putting on a tie and showing up at 9:00 a.m.? ... $550! ... and this in 1999! The height of the American empire! ... grammar school kids with cell phones that take pictures. Everyone with TVs THIS BIG ... and SUVs even bigger ... the bigger and more expensive the better. That is the enduring motto.

Do you know what $275 a week gets you on Long Island?

A fucking bitchy girlfriend!

Headaches!!!!

Heartache!!!!!

Definitely no pussy!!!! … watch it walk by day and night. I was getting fat. Like a eunuch.

I had plenty of weed though! And I learned to write a headline, sort of. I learned where the commas go.

Personally, the money didn't bother me and the job had its perks. Everyone's happy to see a reporter … usually.

Aside from the occasional perp walk or county official getting caught with his hand in the cookie jar … lots of smiling faces. Lots of opening doors, big meals and parting gifts … and always snacks and soft drinks.

Lots of time out of the office, too.

Nights when I had to cover city hall meetings, every other Tuesday … I could split by lunch. Take a surf. I was highly encouraged to be out and about.

I was a favorite at the Jewish Community Center. I found it refreshing. Previously, I had only rolled with "non practicing" Jews. They made it very clear.

Not Joey V!

I walked in on him one morning … two little boxes strapped to his shoulders. Another to his head. He was tuning into Neptune.

He tried explaining it to me, the Tefillin. We agreed on God but differed on Israeli politics.

I spent a day on the Long Beach pier fishing with handicapped kids. The local bait shop sponsored it — a true old school angler who wanted to share his passion with the dilapidated gangster generation. Pants nearly at their knees…. even in wheelchairs.

Maybe.

Or maybe he just got back from the annual Bait Shop Convention … they put two and two together … Wheelchairs. Sitting around pier side. A couple rods and reels.

I interviewed the head Freemason on Long Island … this before I knew they were Luciferians. He made it sound so appealing … belief in *a* God and a tuxedo … I couldn't afford the tux.

The only bitch was election night. At the polls for however long it took … drive back to the office at 10:00 p.m. with the breaking news. Bang out the results. Submit the story … Get it kicked back … these editors are never satisfied … It's like moving heavy equipment with someone watching over your shoulder: "Just a little bit more over there."

It's easy for them. They don't start their day with a blank page.

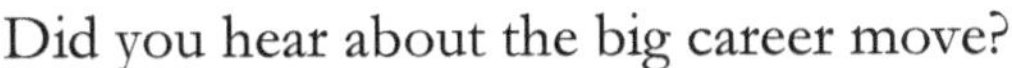

Did you hear about the big career move?

After answering a few phony baloney Help Wanted ads — headhunters tricking me into Midtown Manhattan to test my typing and editing skills — I caught a break. I wizened up. I made sure to ask, "Is this for an actual job interview?"

I wasn't nervous. I couldn't possibly be more unaccomplished having graduated with a 3.75 GPA. Right on the cusp of Magna Cum Laude and Cum Laude … I told my editor I was going to cover something at city Hall and slipped into Manhattan once again. Always back to Manhattan.

This potential new publisher, Rick Telberg, boy was he excited to see me. He must have really been in a bind … he politely feigned interest in my pathetic portfolio. The local fires. The crippled anglers. Interviews with former Long Beach lifeguard and New York State Assemblyman Harvey Weisenberg. I even had a picture with Hillary Clinton when she came to suck up to the only democratic town in Nassau County … Actually, don't call it a town. The City of Long Beach! …. they make it very clear. Very self-conscious: Fifteen blocks long, four blocks wide … every decent hurricane and the little city sandbar goes bye-bye.

Accounting Today … he wanted to know if I had any familiarity with the subject. I confessed the debit/credit brainteasers sent me running to English Lit. 101.

He still didn't care. It didn't matter … as long as I could rewrite a press release and kind of edit copy. As long as nothing too atrocious got by.

Then came the big question: would I accept $18,850 a year plus benefits?

Would I!

$725 every two weeks … o'boy were my pockets going to be fat!

Amie wasn't impressed. She didn't bail right away, but within two weeks she's packed and ready to go. Back to her mother's place. Anyplace but this sinking ship.

I remember sitting back against the apartment's brick base and watching her load up her truck. The one with the Bob Marley and Grateful Dead stickers … I remember watching her start it without a care in the world, head up the road and pull a U-ey at the end of the block … I remember all the large Tupperware-like containers she had stuffed in the back of her Cherokee, and how much shit was in them and thinking, "Her parents bought her that Jeep."

It didn't take long for Amie's mom to call. Two, three days and the "Amie loves you. Amie misses you" started coming in … who wouldn't miss a freezer full of weed and a hang out for freeloading friends?

I was still too in a daze — shaken and wounded psycholog-ically, alone — to consider my real position: Young! Free! Single! Beachfront pad!

But the veterans at *Accounting Today* were getting nervous. Little comments that weren't encouraging … about declining advertising sales. About getting their resumes in order.

Then word came down that the office was closing. That we'd be moving in with our parent company, Thomson Financial, at the World Trade Center.

That didn't sound so good … an additional 45 minutes of underground subway time added to my already 90-minute morning commute.

Once again, I'm scouring the Sunday New York Times.

Ah, an opening at Hearst … an operation I've actually heard of … Citizen Kane … a Long Island branch only 30 minutes from Long Beach … by car, which I didn't have. But what's with minor details?

I find my way to their office. I'm not impressed. It's a dump. The cargo bay doors give it away … definitely a former warehouse. I know one when I see one. I'm qualified.

Again, the executive editor must be in a jam. He's telling me about the travel … free trips to Las Vegas, to Germany… he doesn't know I don't like to fly.

He tells me about the pretty public relations women. The gifts. The industry recognition … he likes that I like jazz.

He sells me on the publisher … Cuban! That's a plus. And a black belt in karate! Double plus!!

I can see myself fitting in. He wants me to take a couple issues home. He jams them in my hands as he shows me the door. He scoots me out. The conversation's over.

I sneak a quick peak while exiting the lobby: *Floor Covering Weekly* … You got to be fucking kidding me.

No, it's no joke. And Amie's back at the apartment but not for long … she's heading off to Israel with some Jewish friends. And then to Colorado to snowboard … she's really having fun.

Why not? School's out. Five years at the two-year Nassau Community College … she was in no rush. The long-term plan.

Floor Covering Weekly loved my ideas … there's only so many dopes that will work for $20,000 a year. They wanted me to start right away. Right after signing a document freeing Hearst of any future liability associated with asbestos-related health claims made on my behalf.

Amie was signing some documents of her own, too. She, Jed and a few of his band mates were going to partner on a three-bedroom apartment on the opposite side of town.

Right before the coup, before I knew what was up, Amie calls me on my way to work … a plane crashed into the World Trade Center.

I stick my head out the bus window … crystal clear! … blue sky! … a Cessna pilot must have had a heart attack, a seizure.

I get to the office and think we've all been canned, that they're shutting down the entire operation. No more *Floor Covering Weekly*.

Faces full of panic.

Standing room only in the conference room.

… I'm thinking, "Here we go again. Time to scramble for another job."

But no!

Everyone's huddled together. Solidarity in defeat before the TV looping footage of the planes crashing. Anchormen commentary as the smoking buildings continue to tower over the skyline from the helicopter wide-angle shot.

Live street-level footage of New Yorkers crying, bawling their eyes out. New Yorkers panicked. New York at its most confused … then the buildings fell and there was a terrifying silence.

PART III:

WAKING UP

CHAPTER 13:

A SEAT FOR EVERY ASS

"Therefore, my dear friends, as you have always obeyed — not only in my presence, but now much more in my absence — continue to work out your salvation with fear and trembling."— Philippians

There's nothing more pathetic than taking your ex's shit to her new place, partly out of love, partly to sneak a peek of the situation … I got a good glimpse all right. I got a good fucking look … Jed skedaddling from one room to the next before answering the door.

I surprised everyone! Real early! … made it seem like I was on my way back from a surf: "You guys paddle out?"

Yeah, I could tell by his hair and the crud in his eyes that he had just fallen into a deep sleep. A nice peaceful slumber. Intoxicated on liquor, drugs and new ass … well, new ass for him at least … good ol' buddy ol' pal … after months mooching weed and pizza rolls over at my one-room, dilapidated, beach-side Ramada Inn.

Amie's up and involved now … Jed scuttles back to the room he darted to before answering the door; he's unaware I caught his little musical chairs act, his tippy-toes dance routine.

Now I'm the one in Amie's room … I see the djembe and surfboard I bought her. One's a coffee table. The other's a coat rack in the corner.

I'm wasting my time, belittling myself with the "how could you" routine.

Ridiculous!

Loser! … both of us; she just didn't know it yet.

The anger! At myself! For not punching Jed out! For loving such an ungrateful, spoiled, misdirected soul! … it simmers in me for a few months. It helps burn off the extra pounds I packed on. And then I get the call … little brother is getting married. It's time to come home.

I admit there was proper notice … well in advance! I have to give them that … marked on the calendar! Best Man! Have to be there! … Only problem … No car. Three feet of snow and the Long Island Rail Road calls it quits … No trains out. No trains in.

Wait, there's a break in the weather. Father Christmas is coming a couple weeks early … they'll run a few trains until 6:00p.m. After that, you're on your own. Good luck. Maybe a return trip. Maybe not. It's up to you if you feel lucky.

I rubber band shopping bags around the only shoes I own. It's snowing so hard the city's not bothering with the side streets. Even the plows can't get through.

A hat on my head. A scarf around my face. A backpack with pajamas … the good news is that the snow is thick! No slush! Just mounds and mounds of snow! I'm crawling over snowdrifts … it takes 45 minutes to traverse the three blocks to the train station.

Nobody on the road; I'm the only lunatic on the train … choo choo. The tracks are literally ablaze. Small fires rising up every 20 yards. It's the only way ... who knew that existed? Little Sternos, Bunsen Burners built into the track.

An hour and a half later: Penn Station. Like a ghost town! The city that never sleeps my ass! Everyone catching zzzzs but me.

I step out onto Seventh Ave. and it's beautiful ... the city of greed is pure white. Silent. Redeemed ... the snow's crunching under my feet as I hoof it another two blocks to the PATH station ... I'm in luck again. It's running. We're burrowed underground until Jersey City's Journal Square. Then it's me and a handful of homeless crazies around a space heater ... I'm waiting for a connecting train ... they're waiting for their own private miracles.

I pull a frozen quarter out of my pocket ... it's not enough. I fish out another one ... boop, boop, boop. "I'll be in Harrison in an hour. The train leaves in 45 minutes."

"You'll have to take a cab; the roads are too bad" ... That's my dad. First words in two years ... my sister did visit once; to my miniscule beach abode. She couldn't come back; said it pained her to see me living that way ... tell me about it.

I say goodbye to my little bum friends. I leave them there playing paddy cake over the furnace. I'm on the PATH. I'm on the last leg of the journey ... I see where I used to turn off to go to Saint Peters ... Wow! A world away! ... I see where Rob crashed the car, where Jack Gilmore got killed. I see a couple miles of parked containers, sketchy warehouses and toxic marshland ... where they occasionally fish out Mafia roadkill.

"Harrison!" ... that's my stop. I don't understand why the conductor's shouting. I'm the only one on the train. Well, it's just the two of us.

It's dark. The driving snow muffles the platform light fixtures.

The cabstand's open when I get downstairs, but the dispatcher makes it perfectly clear: no rides.

"How long?"

It's not a matter of length … time nor distance. The snow's too deep … There're no drivers. No cabs. He's only there to answer the phone as a courtesy.

I stick my freezing hand into my pocket … when you have no cell phone you better weigh yourself down with quarters. For the PATH train turnstiles. For moments like this.

Boop. Boop Boop … "Dad, I need a ride. There're no taxis."

He tells me to wait it out. Maybe the snow will let up and the cabs will come back … it's difficult to explain things to him. He doesn't handle conflict well.

I stand around in the snow. It's piling up on me. I better keep moving … I pace left. I pace right. A train goes by overhead heading back to Jersey City … I start thinking.

Boop. Boop. Boop … "Dad, there're no cabs. They're closed. There's nobody here."

He tells me he doesn't know what to do.

I get a bright idea.

"Why don't one of you come and get me! It's only a couple miles."

He's not having it. There's no way … he'd rather me walk the five or six miles.

I set out. At least the first couple miles are level … That's what I'm thinking. I am the Best Man after all.

A quarter mile in, I hit the Quick Check … I go in for hot cocoa. A Snickers. It's already been a long night.

Boop. Boop. Boop … my future sister-in-law answers.

Now I'm getting somewhere.

Someone reasonable.

A beautiful Irish girl, she's working two jobs while putting herself through Grad School … she appreciates family. I tell her I'm sorry,

I'm going to miss the engagement party. I'm turning back. I'm going home while I can.

Now they're coming to get me.

I think about Julio's fat ass and his Ford Explorer. Him and my sister and dad all warm watching cable TV.

I think of my brother and his fucking new yellow Xterra … he's definitely cracking jokes at my expense. Mr. Wisenheimer.

The problem with our country becomes evident … we have no more men. What we have are males with powerful SUVs but weak constitutions. No courage … and the men with balls: no brains! We ran out of wisdom a long time ago!

Here comes Kathy pulling into the lot. Easy to spot her … the only headlights in town.

The streets actually aren't that bad over here. The ride's not long enough to diffuse my rage … While I'm unsnapping my rubber band and shopping bag galoshes: "You fucking assholes are gonna make me walk?"

Now I'm the downer. I spoil the jovial mood.

Before the snow on my head melts, Kathy has me back in her jalopy. The lowest riding, oldest and least reliable of the bunch … I'm back on the train platform waiting … the lights of downtown Newark are gleaming and reflecting off the Passaic River … It's calm. It's beautiful. But I know it's an illusion. I lived there too long to be fooled.

I get my first overseas assignment. I'm not happy about it … I'm flying west to Chicago to meet Claes Wennerth, CEO of the Sweden-based Alloc Corporation, and a small group of reporters … we'll all be flying east again, back over New York and the Atlantic to Copenhagen. But I'm getting ahead of myself.

Ten o'clock at night and I'm uncharacteristically comfortable fastened to the fuselage. Clear skies. I can see stars and other planes off in the distance. Best of all, my headset has a special channel tuned to the cockpit … it's a nice feature.

"Pittsburgh, this is 505. We're at 30,000 feet … smooth ride … all is well and God is with us."

The tower rang back good news. Other planes' cockpits, tuned to the same channel, confirmed: God was with us. No worries. No turbulence.

A reassuring sense of safety came over me … all this communicating. We weren't flying blind into the black after all. Or we were and it was all right.

One a.m. and we land at O'Hare.

Before I could tuck myself away into a corner, I'm ambushed by Matt Spieler, the lead writer for *Floor Covering News*, our magazine's closest competitor … he wants to discuss his bad back. It'll be the same story for the next ten years … the car accident. It wasn't his fault. The pills.

Do I want one?

"Yes please!"

If I didn't like to iron, this Matt Spieler — about 10- to 15 years older, balding with a ponytail — he's the Maharishi Ghandi of not giving a fuck. Permanently wrinkled!

Here's another journalist. Darius Helm. He's with *Floor Focus*. A classier rag but they're not really in the same market as us. He's more about the architect and designer. We're all about the specialty retailer.

Darius is classier too. He's handsome. Clean cut but with a gold tooth … something about growing up in Spain, England and the Middle East. An internationally-oriented family. Anyway, on him the shiny tooth is more charming than ghetto.

Wait. There's Claes! He's taking us to Viken to see his research and development lab. They're revolutionizing the laminate floor business … mechanical locking … no more glue! Just *clickety-click*… presto change-o and your floor's installed. Anybody can do it … Well, nearly anybody.

His competitors don't believe him. But that's what we're for. The press … a few ads and page one stories. We'll convince everybody!

Thank God, he's not in the mood to talk either … how do you think we feel? We just detoured across the country to pick his ass up. On top of that I'm extraordinarily thirsty … it must be the tiny pink pill.

We pile on to yet another plane.

"Can I get a bottle of water, please?"

I'm tucked in against the window … with the pillow and the covers … sip sip. night night.

Next thing I know: coming in for a landing!

Suns up!

More clear skies!

Breakfast is being served!

I better not dilly-dally. They're going to take the fruit and crackers away. We really are losing altitude … there's the ground. Little patches of farm. Not many trees … I wasn't expecting many if these fuckers are half as axe happy as we are. Not with their extended history. More than one volume.

We're on the ground but it's not Sweden. There's still more traveling to do … Claes is an informative guide … he's going to drive us in. He knows the way. Eight trips a year, minimum. He doesn't mind. It's his homeland.

An hour of countryside driving … now there's some trees. Covered in snow. White picket fences too … it's like a vast Christmas wonderland in a dreamy old America. Before the greed set in.

We make it to Helsingborg, an ancient Swedish port city. You can see the ships coming and going … There's an immense castle tower and precipice. Built into its base is our place, where we'll be staying ... I'm amazed it has an elevator. I'm a little skeptical. Certainly not the latest technology.

I'm the last one out. Top floor. A slanted attic ... the bellhop has the courtesy to make a remark; he's glad he's not staying up here.

"Really. Why's that?"

"The last woman to stay on this floor wound up sleeping in the lobby; she refused to come back up. It's haunted ... we had to pack her luggage and bring it down."

We're both hunched over making our way through the tiny corridor. He leaves me at a diminutive door. It's like a doll's house ... I was too tired to be terrified.

I slept through lunch and dinner. I caught so many zzzzs Casper could have been playing the trombone ... I wouldn't have known a thing. But now I'm up early, antsy and hungry ... it's still sort of dark out.

I bundle up. They weren't kidding about the cold ... it's just me, the seaport and the castle tower ... this place was definitely expecting company, that's for sure. A stone's throw across the Baltic: Denmark! A little further: Germany, Poland, Lithuania, Finland ... no wonder ghosts are prancing around the neighborhood.

Our host was being generous: "Meet in the lobby at 11:30a.m."

That's a break. Usually when these bastards buy the flight and hotel ... forget it! They got you by the balls! They want to whisk you away to here and there. Early starts! Plant tours! Corporate offices! Lunches! Dinners! ... doesn't matter what city you're in. It's all the same. You don't see a thing except what they put in front of your face.

Not this time! ...   I'm out the door. My head's down and I'm shivering in my wool jacket … this would've been a good time for gloves. I squeeze my muscles to stay warm. I consider going back. Everything is closed along the ancient cobblestone streets. The sun is just peaking over the horizon. It's fighting to make a difference.

Wait!

What's this?

Could it really be?

… 3,828 miles from New York: The Golden Arches! … the only place open! There's steam pouring out the door.

I saw Pulp Fiction. It spared me the metric-system culture shock … no quarter pounders with cheese … what I wasn't prepared for was the ravishing beauty!

The girl wrestling with the greasy fryer: a total knockout! In New York she wouldn't have to lift a finger! Same with the girls at the register and mopping up the back … I wonder if this place has any rideable surf, about applying for a green card.

I'm back on the street. It's finally light out. A little further recon-naissance and I'm away from the castle walls. No more cobblestones. Now I'm in the future … ultra modern architecture. Lots of sharp angles, polished metal.

I stick my face in another window … oops, I've been spotted. It's awkward. To make it better I walk in, I sit down ... Another hottie! This one's older and has scissors ... Before I know it: she lops off my ponytail. I got a clean-shaven face … bye bye goatee. She tells me I'm handsome … I haven't heard that in a while. I realize the hap-py-go-lucky hippy look and the I'm-in-a-relationship potbelly wasn't doing much for me … especially since I really wasn't that happy, no longer in a relationship.

I double-time it back to the hotel. The morning was getting away from me … there's no getting around flooding the joint. The shower is too tiny; there's no curtain. Only half a glass door that's fixed in place … I use up every towel and washcloth … it doesn't matter. The water seeps out across the cramped quarters. I'm like a clumsy, reckless giant in this attic space.

I get down to the lobby a few minutes early. Everyone's already there. A bunch of overachievers … they notice my little make over. We focus on that rather than Matt Spieler being the only one not wearing a suit. He didn't feel like it … Maybe it was his back. He's in scrubs and a lumberjack flannel … it's an interesting choice.

We pile into a touring van. Claes is taking us to the R&D center to meet Darko Pervan; the brains, the inventor and financier of the operation … he's the one paying for all of this.

Clickety clack… yup, it works! These glueless locking floors … even I could do it. Just a little help.

Darko explains the patents … they'll sue everybody! The licensees will have to pay! Obviously, a better method! It will completely revolutionize the industry!

If he says so.

I know the deal: definitely agree! Keep any critiques to yourself! Wait until you're back in the office, or at least on the plane.

Now I'm in Darko's personal Mercedes … they prefer our magazine. We're heading through the Black Forest to his country estate for Saint Lucia's Day … it's sort of their pre-Christmas celebration. They kick things off a little early.

What a place! Personal movie theater! Eight car garage! … and the spots aren't vacant. Each car more impressive than the last … he's flown in lobster and caviar just for us … plus all the local cuisine; the cheeses and fish these guys are into. So much food and booze! A bona fide feast!

Yeah, these CEOs got it good. Don't doubt that for a second.

⚬⚬⚬

Fortunately for us journalists, Claes had two days of meetings to sit through. He thought it best if we just stayed put in Helsingborg … I liked his thinking.

Casper let me sleep in again, too. Not a peep. Not a single "booo."

I head to the castle's dining room … Real fancy! Wood walls! Very ornate furniture! … but boy did they have some ugly old carpeting. They could use some of Claes' clickety-clack flooring.

What a buffet … tiny! diminutive! No wonder these fuckers were so skinny. Instead of bacon and sausage … thin slices of cheese and raw salmon. I kind of dig it. It's better than burnt pig flesh … not really. But I'm willing to try.

I run into Darius and Matt. They got a big scheme going, they planned a little class trip for themselves. They're taking a ferry back to Copenhagen. They've been tuned to Christiana, an autonomous commune community with legal hash and weed. A real hush hush Amsterdam on the other side of the Baltic. Nothing to it. An hour ferry and short train ride … gurgle, gurgle, gurgle. Down go the bong hits.

I didn't trust their plan. I couldn't afford a conviction, especially on this side of the Atlantic while on the job. I was already on thin ice. A high-wire act with no safety net … no fucking up: that was my mantra.

I ask if they can bring some back. I wouldn't mind creating a few floating apparitions of my own in that attic … "No way!" … They were pretty clear about it. They didn't want to push their luck.

I'm on my own. At the end of the block is the Karnan Tower, what's left of the original castle. A true rook … magnificent but boarded up tight. They don't want visitors. I can imagine why … with how dark and gloomy it is around here … a perfect spot to take a final plunge! Romantic! … If I had a little Christiana stash I'd turn it into my personal chimney.

More icy cobblestones. An Old World basement pub … it's pretty lively. A young college crowd on holiday … Bottoms up! …There's a DJ in one corner. A blackjack table in the other … I spend a few Kroner on drink, a few more at the table.

They're definitely curious about me. They don't see many Americans; at least not in person. Their prior experience: 100 percent TV … I'm an instant celebrity. Doesn't matter that I write for a two-bit flooring magazine. They want to practice their English. They want to size me up … one of the girls take me outside. I warm my hands on her ass before going back for another round.

Now we all pile out together … we're good buddies holding each other up; the cobblestones are extra slippery.

They take me to the train station. Very Modern. I'd rather stay in antiquity, but you have to trust the locals … especially the young hot ones nibbling on your neck.

I tell them about Matt and Darius. Their trip to Christiana … Now I've done it. They're looking at me like I'm a junky; they get suspicious … it's time to finish my drink and split. I can catch a drift.

It doesn't matter. I can find my scene in any city. I know where to look … the docks are always a good starting point. Not right on the water, but a block or two in … regardless, the water calls me. I'm sitting on the edge of the Baltic with a pen and a pad but have nothing to write about … I just think about my mother. Then how the piers of Helsingborg, Manhattan, Jersey City and Newark are all the same at night: Lonely. Cold. Sad … a place for disturbed people who don't want to be disturbed.

Sure enough, two blocks away I see a line forming outside a nondescript warehouse … BINGO!!!! I know I found it.

Standing in line in front of a few young blondes, I let my passport flop in the breeze a bit. It does the trick. They initiate conversation … I'm a fast learner. With these two on my hip I'm sure to get in … clear the way for the American!

They go to coat check and I head to the bar ... without weed or ecstasy I have to pile on the Red Bulls and Vodka.

Now my pen wants to write!

Now I'm a chatterbox in the corner, on some plush ultramodern upholstery.

In this fancy place, with all these beautiful people ... I look ridiculous. Writing poetry in public is always ridiculous.

I look up. I notice one of the Barbie Twins on the dance floor ... She's making her way towards me. There's unmistakable eye contact but it's not awkward. I'm too far from home and drunk to be awkward.

She tells me she's leaving.

Again, I'm no rocket scientist but I can take a hint ... weed? ... not a mention! Going to keep my mouth shut this time.

Her and her friend. They're hanging on to both arms while we traverse the slip-n-slide streets ... too bad for the socialism, a personal injury lawyer could really clean up in this town.

Lucky me. I'm escorting them back to the train station. I learned the way. My almost dance partner, Sofie, she doesn't have to say a thing. She can just keep kissing me. I have a lot in common with her dad ... he's locked away in an insane asylum.

———∼∼∼———

I'm back in time for real Christmas ... well, Christmas with the family anyway. They asked my brother to invite me. He doesn't believe in God, Jesus or Santa Claus ... he's just keen on gifts. Who wouldn't be?

Apparently, me, that's who ... the Grinch!

"I'll come for dinner but no presents." I make it clear. I have my reasons.

That's not good enough for them … not to disregard tradition. They want detailed explanations. I'm going to have to spell it out … I try my best. It would help if they read scripture. A little history … more than a light once over; a Roman-Catholic "I told ya so."

Shepherds outside tending their flocks in December?

No way! … Strictly an indoor affair! … even in Bethlehem: 40 degrees and below.

Angel Gabriel?

He's instructing Mary, he's strongly advising: "Eat some dates!"

… only available in late spring!

I don't expect Americans to get the reference. The Qu'ran … if it's not Jesus, Buddha, Adam Smith or Lucifer: zero interest! … not with all those channels to choose from.

The whole shebang: Christmas tree, wreath, mistletoe and yule log … totally pagan! 100 percent so!

December 25?

Roman festival of the sun god!

A special day set aside for Baal!

There's a reason the Vatican's in Rome; that mass is held on "Sun" day … a gentle blending. A nudge. Easing the pagans and Christians together. Crossbred Catholicism … Constantine knew what he was doing at Nicaea.

The family doesn't want to hear it … historical facts or not … "opium for the masses" … That guy was right! He was playing the correct tune!

Regardless, I have to start my own journey, my own little pilgrimage … there's no guiding star. Not with this smog. I just follow the tracks. Here we go again … the Long Island Rail Road from Long Beach to Jamaica. A little switcheroo and another train to Penn Station.

There's no snow this time. Just lots of people … with gifts! Everyone's weighed down real good!

Not me. I'm light as a feather bustling over to the P.A.T.H. train.

The line to the World Trade Center is still down … it's pretty disturbing. New York hasn't gotten its bounce back … and definitely suspicious of Arabs! Hindus! Anyone with a turban, really.

I'm in luck … the train to Newark is waiting. The doors are open. Here comes the moment of truth: I pull out my cell phone … a new gadget courtesy of Hearst Publishing … it's a bit of a compromise. On both our parts … since those towers fell: company-wide freeze on pay raises … I was lucky to have a job … my publisher made that abundantly clear. Still, I had to eat … and I wasn't exactly keen on all the recent flying … not with those Arabs down there. I'd seen Discovery Channel. I knew what those Stinger Missiles could do.

Boop. Boop. Beeb. Boop … they're coming to get me! They learned the lesson! They'll meet me at the Harrison Station.

They make me wait, though … they don't leave right away. Why would they? Z100 can only play so many hits in 10 minutes … why risk being early?

Ho! Ho! Ho! It must be Christmas … there's my dad! In a new Lexus! A Christmas gift to himself.

Thank God it's only a 10-minute ride … just enough time for pleasantries.

He's not surprised Amie left. Or that I didn't have a car … he definitely told me so. He warned me pretty good about keeping that UPS sales job.

We're home. Well, his home … everyone's there … My sister and her husband Julio; my brother Chris and his fiancé … Abuela almost faints when she sees me. She's thanking God and Jesus at the same time.

Suzanne, my father's girlfriend, and her kids, they're there too … why let Judaism and my mother's corpse get in the way? Why be inconvenienced?

There's plenty of food! That's for sure!

Paella with lobster, two varieties of sweet potatoes — my sister and Suzanne's little passive feud; their own cold war — stuffed mushrooms, cranberries, pork, stuffing, plantanos, baked ziti and lasagna … there's bread stacked a mile high … red wine *and* sangria … no wonder everyone's so fat. Except my brother … his hair has gone the way of his faith. He's compensated with über abbs … marathons, biking, rock climbing. Go, go, go. The more coffee the better. He brought a bucket full from Dunkin Donuts.

Well, it's time to hang the stockings … Tradition! … Abuela first. Then daddy, then Nicole, then me, then Chris. Descending order! … and now the additions: Julio, Kathy and Suzanne … I can tell Suzanne's a last-minute decision … a regular sock. Not too stained … some things are best left unsaid. Her kids have the good sense and manners to decline … the lobster, the pork … there's only so many rabbinical laws to break in a day.

I was feigning joviality … I went so far as to recommended Easter in Florida. Like the good ol' days. For old times sake.

A resounding silence!

I had no idea why, but I could tell I shoved my foot in my mouth! I really said something I shouldn't have. Touched upon a taboo.

"Dad sold the houses; he put the money in the stock market with Suzanne's friend."

Merry Christmas! Now there's a stocking stuffer!

Good thing my dad knows nothing about the stock market … going all in right at the height of the dot.com bubble … every pyramid scheme has its last sucker. Buy high, sell low.

Now he blames Bin Laden ... he thinks the money went away. That it evaporated ... I don't have the heart to fill him in. That he passed it to someone else. A quantitative easing for the wealthy; for Suzanne's stockbroker buddy.

CHAPTER 14:

EUREKA!!!

"Sex is full of lies. The body tries to tell the truth. But, it's usually too bat-tered with rules to be heard, and bound with pretenses so it can hardly move. We cripple ourselves with lies." — Jim Morrison.

When I'm done with you, you'll know all about flooring … the ceramic tile … the hardwood … the laminate, vinyl, linoleum, carpet, area rugs and cork ... the industry was booming! … $24 billion in U.S. sales alone! The result of what experts called "the cocooning effect."

Since those towers went down … nobody wants to fly. No Disneyland. No Grand Canyon. No Las Vegas or Europe. Everyone's staying put! Everyone's taking a second mortgage and buying new floors.

Mohawk, Shaw, Mannington, Anderson, BR-111 … they couldn't cut the rainforest down fast enough! … Exotic woods here and there! The more expensive and shinier the better! Brazilian Cherry. Mahogany … Brazil or Africa, it didn't matter… as long as it didn't come from the U.S! … and that it was expensive! That's what mattered most!

At 5:00 a.m. I'm on a train to meet my executive editor Steve Feldman and his cunt assistant Alycia. They can both afford cars.

We pile into Steve's Lexus SUV. He knows he's fortunate. He's making over $100,000 at a rag like *Floor Covering Weekly* ... *Floor fucking Covering Weekly!!!!!*

Of course, this doesn't humble him. He flaunts it ... he's right up there with my dad. With the, "We're not here for a long time. We're here for a good time," mentality.

Alycia revels in it. She knows she's going to be taking a lot of free rides ... to fancy places. She's going to put back some fine food and wine on someone else's dime.

One hour in traffic with these two to go 10 miles on the Belt Parkway ... I've never been so happy to see the Verrazano Bridge! ... by the time we're in Jersey, on 95 South: I sound like a broken record ... "Oh yeah?" ... "Really?" ... I was going along. Doing my best to keep it pleasant ... they were really enthralled about American Idol, Survivor and the Mets. They kept bringing up their outdoor gas grills and Texas Hold 'em ... I didn't want to get voted out of the car.

They definitely didn't want to discuss how Bush stole the election. Or how his family funded Hitler and Osama Bin Laden ... were very close, business partners actually, with the Hinckleys ... the irony ... about John Hinckley ... and daddy Bush being vice president when Reagan took an explosive projectile to the ribcage ... Well, they really do know a lot of people. The Bushes.

Down in South Jersey, off the Turnpike, it's nothing but wetlands ... looks like decent fishing and waterfowling ... a couple turns ... over the tracks and a long zigzagging driveway ... There's Mannington! ... a huge compound! ... multiple factories and administrative buildings.

Out front of the main office? ... a mini wetlands ... artificial ... fake waterfall and pond. A plaque commemorating their commitment to the environment ... what's a little polyvinylchloride? A little phthalate? ... it's my job to know but not report ... our industry's little secret … no real harm … as long as you don't ingest, take a good whiff.

They roll out the red carpet. Our names are lighted up on a board behind the reception desk … They waste no time. Right to a private dinning room for a four-course meal. We let Steve do all the talking. He's the veteran … now Alycia's following my lead with the "uh-huhs." She's run out of bullshit to say.

After they fill our bellies it's time for the main event, to see their new products … I'm paying attention. You know who is gonna have to right the story when we get back … they flatter me. My ability to quickly turn around copy. Accurate. Quality … Mannington's a big advertiser. They didn't invite us down for nothing.

Steve's not dragging out the goodbyes. He's itching to get out of there, too … they're sticking farewell goodie bags under our arms. They're weighing us down as we go.

We're back on 95, the Turnpike … we're making good time. That's what not dillydallying will do for you. We can beat the traffic home.

But now Steve's on the phone with the "Yeah. Yeah. Sure… that would be great."

I'm watching A-10 Warthogs flying in formation out the window as he finishes up with the call … Do we want to "stop off" for dinner? … Do we want to meet the public relation's gal from Armstrong? … In Philadelphia? … he's really dispersing the details.

No!

Definitely not!!!

An hour and a half out of the way in each direction!!!!!!

"Are you paying for drinks?" That's what Alycia wants to know.

Four hours later, she's passed out in the back seat. Steve's in and out of consciousness … he's mumbling about how he hates his wife. He's in love with other women … I noted the plurality.

For a finale he tells me about his father, and how he died while he was young and how he coped with it by doing coke and partying … No wonder our nation's GDP is going through the roof. Construction, publishing, the presidency … everyone's all jacked up.

Back in my office, it's difficult to make a deadline … unknown coworkers from other divisions knocking, constantly interrupting asking for donations … for bridal and baby showers … to sign Get Well cards … to have cake and sing happy birthday to other unrecognizable coworkers. It's amazing we can publish anything.

I never set out to be a fighter, or more appropriately a poorly paid punching bag, a hack. In fact, Master Chan made it clear from the beginning: "Don't be a fighter. Be a beater."

I left the Long Island Kung Fu Academy while I was still with Amie. They taught me the rudiments of Wing Chun … intercepting and sticking to an attack; using the adhesion to compile data, the attacker's intention, momentum. But what these guys really loved to do: forms!

The more forms the better!

And if we weren't training forms or playing ring-around-the-rosy with Chi Sau, we were lion dancing. One man under the bamboo-framed head jumping left and right, opening and closing the mouth, blinking the eyes … another man in the back flapping the body's cape up and down like a lunatic.

The important thing: staying low and hunched over! … the teacher said it built our legs and Kung Fu.

What it really did was build his bank account.

Chinese New Year, weddings, any Asian restaurant opening in Nassau County … there we were: banging drums, twirling fake weapons and prancing around in our lion costume. Semi-martial marionettes.

One evening a former "disciple" shows up … these guys can get pretty cultish. But this stranger, he's not all glassy eyed over sifu. At least not any more … I can tell his days of phony baloney are behind him. I know a capable fighter when I see one.

He's older than the rest of us. He's older than the few remaining disciples that grace us with their presence from time to time … He's got to be at least 45. Probably closer to 50 … sifu's willing to let him demonstrate a few moves. He's going to show us a little something he learned from "an old man in Chinatown."

We're impressed by the apparent simplicity and effectiveness. But now he wants to know if any of the disciples want to spar, throw on the boxing gloves and see it for real … ha … that's a good one.

A mere mention of sparring from me in the past, a suggestion … a deluge of reverse psychology! … they were doing me a favor! I was insulting them! I was putting myself in danger!

After a while, I had enough … I couldn't take any more of the Crouching Tiger, Hidden Dragon routine. I wanted to see a little more Mike Tyson and a little less Jackie Chan.

I filled them in on a little history. I opened up just a bit … Issin-Ryu black belt … Ni Dan. Second degree … more than 13 years of training. It wasn't an accident this face stayed so cute.

"Sifu" … he makes us address him that way … "I've never seen a martial art school like this where there's no sparring."

That was the last thing anyone wanted to hear! It wasn't good for morale. Or business … it wasn't good for the three or four senior students I grew dizzy bowing to all night long.

Now they're looking back and forth, deciding who's going to take the beating.

After a brief delay — when it's apparent sifu's willing to take the bet on their behalf — the biggest steps forward. They're stacking the odds in their favor.

"We don't train for 'sparring.' I can't guarantee I won't cripple you."

Now he's trying to scare me. He's doing a poor job at bluffing.

When you really want to beat someone's ass … you lure them in. You make them feel they have a good chance. You encourage. Embolden.

"Well, I signed the waiver. If you can't help your power I understand. I'll try my best."

He takes a Kung Fu pose with his hands held out … He circles right. He circles left … He throws a couple heavy shots straight out of the forms … from a safe distance. He's pretty far away … he's really beating up the air.

I don't throw a thing. I just keep turning on my axis … to keep facing him, to keep up with his bouncing around.

Finally, he builds his confidence. He charges … no Kung Fu. No technique … Pure anger! … 100 percent trying to take my head off! Going for the knockout!

His big haymaker creates a HUGE opening!

I unload a sidekick to his ribs … I shuffle-stepped into it. I loaded the hip all the way.

His legs come out from under him.

He bounces a bit. Just slightly … it wasn't in his forms to get back up.

Sifu liked what he saw. Now he's willing to show me the sword form. He wants to spend a little more time … being the way I am, I go out and buy a legitimate broadsword from Kris Cutlery.

Out-on-his-ass wants to see it. He wants to give it a whirl; remind everyone why we bow to him … I have to admit, he moves well for a big guy. Very acrobatic! He does have excellent form!

"Be careful" … I warn him … "It's really sharp" … it really is.

He unsheathes it. He drags his thumb down the blade to help define my relative term "sharp."

At first … nothing! … You can see he's disappointed! He doesn't feel a thing!

Then, his thumb splits like a banana … there's two huge flaps but no blood … he squeezes it. That get's it going. Now we really got some red waterworks … he's out the door without saying goodbye. No saluting … That guy could really move.

So, a few months later when this salt-and-peppered guru showed up to spar, mums the word … everyone starts gathering their fake weaponry; they suddenly have someplace to be. Mass last-minute appointments.

I'm interested in sticking around … my sensei sparred with me when I was six years old. I've sparred with girls, women, grown men and boys. You adjust your power and intensity … Relativity. A well-known concept amongst most martial artists.

We square off.

Sifu's in the corner alternating between a donut, cigarette and coffee … now that everyone else has gone, he doesn't keep up the pretense. He's relaxing. He punched out for the day.

I close in right away. I go for the 1, 2 … a left and a right to test his defenses.

Surprisingly, he steps into it.

Not only does he jam my attack, I'm instantly countered … a decent shot right to my chin. He pulled his power but the point was clear: Too easy.

Alright old man. I won't get so close … I'll take advantage of my youthful legs.

I drive a heavy front kick to his waistline … it's an annoying, disrespectful attack. It prevents him from stepping in and it's low, not so easy to block … if it catches him right, he'll double over … I'll follow up with an uppercut and hook to his noggin … I'd like to see him looking up at me from down there on the vinyl floor tiles … I could teach him a thing or two about that.

He doesn't fall for it. He sort of rides it out … and when I follow with the high round house kick, he actually turns his back to me and kicks up like a donkey while walking away … I take that one on the chin too. Now I'm counting the little twinkling stars. I'm taking in the view of the polyvinylchloride flooring.

Three months! Three months of up and down Canal St. Back and forth across Mott and Mulberry … asking at the martial art supply stores. Accidently popping in on Chinatown sweatshops, gambling dens and whorehouses. Well, mostly accidentally.

I tracked down another of Master Chan's former students, a legitimate Asian who strung me out for a couple free dinners before revealing the location of the 7th floor walk up training hall on Bowery.

I have to say, Master Chan's students weren't exactly Mike Tysons either … mostly Chinese nerds. Every major profession represented … ABC … American born Chinese … bankers, doctors, lawyers … even a goody two-shoes in seminary school. He gave up Buddha for Christ.

His number one student: adopted daughter and disciple little Lisa … Five feet tall, studying to be an architect. She lived and trained with Master Chan. Cleaned his clothes. Cooked his food … we all wondered if there wasn't a little hanky panky going on.

Four days a week, after busing to work, I hop a train from the office to Penn Station … no going outside to sneak a peek at the old *Accounting Today* office building on Seventh Ave. … nope! not this time … only further underground to grab another A, B or C train. Strictly the blue line!

I fumble with tokens to get through the turnstile.

I stand on the piss-soaked platforms amongst every race; every smell of every body odor and food.

I listen to black men rapping out load with headphones on … not everyone has talent.

At the bottom of Canal St. I feel at home.

What used to be The Wetlands is only a few blocks away.

The suits scurry off to their Tribeca and Lower East Side lofts … me and a few thugs head up Canal St., past the fake handbags and watches. Past the "We Buy Gold" signs. Past the audio speakers and fish markets … More people than China! You make better progress walking in the street!

After a few months I found a couple honey holes: One to score rice, two unknown kinds of meat and a Coke for $4 … another for fish balls and noodles … it's best not to think about what you're really getting with these prices … I take my little discount bundle around the block to Roosevelt Park. I watch Latinos and Asians play soccer while sort of developing an appreciation for the game.

With chow time over I skedaddle up Broome St., around the corner to Bowery.

Time for the warm up: seven flights of stairs. In the summer it was dangerous. Stifling.

Up top … in the penthouse … little Lisa's locked herself in behind a super security steal door. I cough. I bang my feet. I shift noisily … Doesn't matter. No one's getting in until 7:30!

Little by little a crowd gathers. We're left looking at each other … I'm the only Round Eye. The only Gwilo.

There's the door! We hear the mechanism tumbling ... very important to salute Lisa properly. She takes it personally.

We file into the training hall. A familiar routine ... the senior students are really beating the hell out of their air!

Their specialty?

Get this.

... walking!

Back and fucking forth.

Can you believe I was constantly corrected? God only knows how I made it up Canal St. ... Good thing teacher wasn't looking.

I'm supposed to be feeling, developing the "connectivity" between my driving back foot, leg, hip and punching arm ... I should feel it spiraling all the way up and out through my strikes.

The more advanced students get to do something special ... they walk themselves dizzy in circles, both arms stretching towards the center's vortex. They look like retarded wind-up Heisman Trophies.

We loved to stand around. Twenty minutes minimum! ... one leg a little further out than the other ... caught mid stride ... with nearly all our weight on the back leg. Boy did we love to do that!

Very important! ... 80 percent of your weight has to be on the back leg!

... and the front arm has to be held out in front just so.

... with the middle finger pointed straight up and lined up with the nose and the palm pushing, yearning out.

The other arm?

Oh, that's top secret. Can't give too much away ... You haven't stood around long enough for that.

I'm not sure why I subjected myself to this.

I remember three days after the towers fell, when I thought it was safe to venture downtown even though Canal St. was full of mine sweeping soldiers, armored vehicles and roadblocks … I looked out the seventh-floor window to where those towers were … I saw their outlines still standing … two rectangular auras beaming in the night.

I saw them for weeks until I was distracted and stopped looking.

It wasn't just Jodi's long slender legs. Or her thin waist and liberally buttoned blouses … it was her scent! She was a young sex machine and knew it. But she hadn't quiet mastered the power, it overwhelmed and often consumed her.

She graduated Phi Beta Kappa from Fordham University in 2001. She was smarter than us … and she knew that too. But since the towers fell there weren't that many jobs for the literary oriented and the flooring business was booming … I already told you, "the cocooning effect" … the second mortgages … the sky-high record home values.

Still, she's only interning. She's losing money on the deal … the great publishing scam! … every kid with a dream of being Woodward and Bernstein … or even worse, my case, a novelist … pennies on the dollar! … College grad for $15,000 a year! … And you better be sharp! … You better be accurate and on time! … Weekly deadlines! Get a typing!

And when you fuck up … Ha! Doctors have it easy! … Their mistakes are buried … Nobody questions them … "Eh, it was their time" … "There was nothing we could do" … they pass the blame. Anybody, anything but their fault.

Us?

It's on the front page!

Bold print!

They call you up. They want you to know they know … they caught you!

"Second column. Third paragraph. Last sentence … see it?"

Yeah. I see it *now*.

I always fault production … They did it! … Somehow it got changed!

Either way, Jodi Lu was now spending more time in Steve's office than Alycia. I couldn't blame Steve.

There was no skirmish or clash or even underlying animosity … Jodi outclassed Alycia in everyway. Especially since Alycia packed on a few pounds after the wedding.

Jodi and I weren't invited.

We got it. We understood. Frankly, neither of us wanted to spend a second more with those people than we needed to.

Instead, we got Taco Bell for lunch. Everyday. I usually wound up paying but it was worth it … I know a good investment when I see it.

Oh, we got to chatting about a great many things.

First and foremost, her doctor boyfriend up in Boston! … she wasn't that into him. The charter flights every weekend … they were losing their charm.

The weekly batches of flowers … one to her, one to her mother … losing their effectiveness! A little too much. A little too overt … it would have been better to leave mommy out of the equation. A little too much too fast.

To top it off, the deal breaker, he was semi-impotent and a bed wetter.

She said she was a virgin in college when she met her last boy-friend. The son of a wealthy psychiatrist in Maine … a bisexual, she said. Well, he blew a few guys.

And his cock? She measured it out for me … from here to there … I don't know how he fit it in her. But he did … she made that abundantly clear.

I asked why she ended it … again, she was very cut and dry: the galoshes!

"I was sick of going up to Maine with his brother tagging along. The both of them with their fucking galoshes."

Fair enough.

The virgin thing, though … kind of splitting hairs. A technicality.

She insisted she was an awkward teen. That she tried to make friends by giving out blowjobs. Hundreds of them! … in the wooded area by her house … in cars … but mostly in the back of Carvel where she worked. How's that for 31 flavors?

We all knew Jodi wasn't going to stay … why would she? There's always something better coming along for a girl like that. Count on it!

Hearst or no Hearst, she wasn't going to work for free forever, no matter how many bylines we gave her.

The higher ups, Steve, thought it would be best to toss her a bone, take her to Surfaces with us … the annual mega trade show held in Las Vegas the week leading up to Super Bowl Sunday.

"We're going to have fun at Surfaces" … that's Jodi making a pronouncement inside my office.

I thought she was naïve … she had no idea how much walking she had in store for herself … a mile every morning just to the convention center. Without stepping outside … and the 7:00 a.m. breakfast meetings? … to ensure no funny business! A good time was definitely not encouraged.

Her jaw's going to drop when she enters that convention hall. She'll be having Carvel flashbacks … 500 yards of floor exhibitions in every direction … Do the math … every house! All of them! … the apartments, skyscrapers, hotels, hospitals, schools, airports … the submarines parked under the Antarctic! … a shit ton of flooring. And more on the way! … forget grass! Its days are numbered.

Nine hours going from booth to booth … faking the "oohs" and "aahs" … seeing the same "exclusive, one of a kind floor" every where you turn … definitely a copy cat industry … Vegas showgirls getting their tits painted … autographs, photos with Dan Marino and Joe Frazier. Mannington spent $50,000 just on their shrimp … those guys know how to have fun.

Wait! Here comes Jodi with a Jack Daniels in her hand!

Do I care to join her?

You bet!

So what I gave up drinking … I've always been good at it. It rewards me. It spoils me.

Here's to Surfaces!

Here's to eking out a living as writers! … well, she wasn't technically getting paid. But down the hatch anyway. Money would never be a concern for her … born with a winning lottery ticket!

~~

Back at the office, you should have seen the Instant Messages Jodi and I were sending each other … William Randolph Hearst would've popped a stiffy.

Nothing overt … we knew Big Brother was watching. There was already a round of layoffs due to "online activity" … I got called in. No surprise there … to see Bill Baker, the head honcho of our little Long Island outpost of misfits … the morbidly obese, stinky, dirty, anorexic and pedophilic … we even had a transsexual stuck in mid-transformation due to lack of funding.

"Ray, there seems to be some suspicious activity on your computer. Visits to some inappropriate sites" … always so polite, politically correct while they're sizing the loop on the noose.

"Well Mr. Baker, I can say that occasionally I'll Google something for work and a sex site pops up, but I don't linger … I got a hot young girlfriend that keeps me more than happy."

We started taking our lunch hour at the park, me and Jodi … that wasn't loose change she was reaching for.

She'd drive me home on nights I didn't go into Chinatown. She was over every chance she got … her not getting along with her mom, not having any friends … definitely worked in my favor!

We smoked joints and poured wine over ourselves. Our own private orgy … she introduced me to new things. She sure was progressive.

It didn't take that long, though. As expected, Jodi flew the coop to Spiegel. They picked her up for pennies as an assistant editor. They even had her do some fit modeling. A two-for-the-price-of-one deal.

For a while she was still showing up in Chinatown. A little topsy-turvy after negotiating seven flights of stairs.

But we started seeing less of each other. She was patronizing certain strategic uptown establishments at happy hour … dating trust fund guys … a few doctors … and then getting semi-serious with a banker … panning … sluicing … dredging … rocker boxing … digging … Gold! … she certainly had a head for funny business.

I was like a prisoner enjoying his last meal. I savored every minute with Jodi knowing the gallows were waiting … it's all smiles and pleasant talk right up 'till the very end … then they drop you and leave you in gravity's hands. How you sway afterwards is your business.

CHAPTER 15:

———⚬~⚬———

FALLING TO IRREVOCABLE DOOM

"Prophet, are you going to worry yourself to death because they will not believe? If We had wished, We could have sent them down a sign from heaven, at which their necks would stay bowed in utter humility. Whenever they are brought a new revelation from the Lord of Mercy, they turn away: they deny it, but the truth of what they scorn will soon hit them." — The Poets, The Qur'an

The best part of being with Jodi — besides the incredible, multi-orgasmic tantric sex; frequent road head; and occasional anal, just to mix it up— was running into Amie while with her. Oh, you should've seen Amie's face with Jodi strutting the boardwalk in a bikini and high heels!

"How'z it going?" ... That's me, surfboard under arm with a grin from here to here ... we must've been taking a break, a little intermission. With Jodi the waves could wait. Passionate sex came first!

... and then we would nap.

We took lots of naps!

136

Jodi wasn't with me for Joe's funeral ... poor guy with his marijuana-green thumb.

He wasn't cut out for this world.

His family and friends were pushing him, though ... into the stock market ... into real estate ... an apprenticeship with a dental technician. He went out and bought all the tools ... a little Dremel Drill and vice. He'd practice and demonstrate for me. His bong and drill ... gurgle, gurgle, gurgle ... bzzzzzz, bbbbzzzzzzzz, bbbbbbbzzzzzzzzzzzz.

They didn't seem like bad gigs. None of them ... I would have jumped all over them.

The day trading option sounded particularly nice. His buddy Amiel would stop by for late-afternoon bong hits and a surf ... "skateboard to work with headphones" ... "keep the headphones on while sitting in front of a computer" ... "make $30,000!" ... "Fuck, make $50,000 to $100,000 a day! A day!"

I was sold.

I already had the skateboarding to work down pat!

"How much money do you need to start? You're playing with your own money, right?" ... that's me being inquisitive. Showing enthusiasm.

The remark blew over ... this opportunity wasn't for me ... strictly non-goyim! Broke Taoists need not apply!

Joey would go all in on Monday — buy the software, a real estate study guide — and retire by Thursday.

Definitely out before Sabbath!

Definitely unemployed before the sun set on Friday!

He took off to Cape Town, South Africa for a three-month surf adventure and left me in charge ... the hidden closet in the bathroom.

Slide the false wall over ... 10- to 15 mature plants in full bloom! With another closet full of little mini-mes ready to take their place.

My job?

Water everybody down! ... daily! ... I had to give everybody a good bath.

Every third day I'd mix in some fertilizer.

It wasn't very hard ... to electrocute myself ... at the rate those plants were going it was inevitable ... the lamps had to be raised! But how?

Looking back now, the random wires hanging out of the ceiling ... I should have known better. I shouldn't have been so lazy. Trying to fasten the lamps to them ... definitely not the way to go!

Joe got back just in time for harvest. He sure did time it right. That's what experience will do for you ... but he's a little off. He's wobbly on his feet.

I wasn't too worried ... I got more than a glimpse of the frozen pounds in his fridge ... my compensation ... little helpings ... but nothing too extravagant.

But then he started missing surf sessions. He stopped training. He was getting more reclusive than usual.

And when I did see him out in the lineup ... Flailing! ... Falling left and right! ... Blowing takeoffs and bottom turns! It was embarrassing.

"Joe. You got to sober up man ... every time I see you, you're wasted."

I was pissing him off. I was being a pain in the ass.

He started getting defensive ... he swore he was only drunk half the times I've accused him.

He started to avoid me. He stopped coming over and answering his door ... Boy was he moody!

James, the old hippy landlord — who knew about Joe's little forest ... the way he subsidized rent — he was ready to kick him out. He was getting too argumentative with Sara, his wife ... it was ruining her pills and vodka high. Who needed it?

A few months later … word from Amiel … Joe passed out at a restaurant in Israel … he hit the deck … BAM! Right out of his chair.

Joe was always advertising Israel. According to him, it was the place to be. He went so far as to say the Mediterranean got good surf … a bit of a stretch … he'd concede when pressed … it wasn't hard. He's surfed the world's best waves and they weren't in Tel Aviv.

Turned out the wobbly feet, the kookiness in the water … the mood swings and the slurred speech: cancerous tumor at the base of his brain! … where the skull connects to the neck!

That sobered everyone up!

I had to fight back the tears when I saw him.

You want to see the zombie invasion? The walking dead? … go to a cancer ward!

In my mind Joe was as good as gone! … I had to carry his hairless body up the stairs into my mini-apartment.

He was optimistic! The chemo was working!

I gave him all the "uh, huhs" I could. I nodded my head. I gently patted his back.

Can you believe he recovered!

He went from a walking corpse with no hair to vibrant … He was skateboarding down the block to check the surf. He was pulling airs out in the lineup.

I admit … on some level I was angry. I was jealous!

How the fuck could he recover from brain cancer? How did the chemo not kill him?

They fried my mother to the bone!! She didn't stand a chance! They must've over cooked her. She went in beautiful and came out well done.

As usual, with me, it had to be the money! That's what people with no money always think!

Are we wrong?

But, less than a year after his recovery, the tumor's back. And this time Joe doesn't want the microwave treatment. He said he'd rather die than go through it again.

His parents fly him down to Florida to see a special nutritionist. He's eating nothing but raw veggies … it's no use. They got to cook him.

A month later I'm at Mount Sinai's hospice center. I wasn't going to make the same mistake I made with my mom … I got my ass to the hospital.

Can you fucking believe it? Just like my mother … the life of the party! The only one who feels like laughing!

"Ray, can you imagine it? Now they're giving me weed and I'm too sick to smoke it."

I'm fucking crushed. I can't accept it. The weed or his impending death.

I'm in the temple at his funeral with the beanie on my head … there's Amie with Jed on the other side of the isle.

"How am I doing now?"

Alone!

No bikinied Jodi. No high heels.

My family doesn't know Joe existed … they don't know me.

They're hanging onto memories of who I was before the world shit all over me … I know … me with my boo hoos. Don't worry! When I'm done with you we'll all have something to cry about. We're all getting slowly cooked. We're all gonna end up well done. You'll see. Your goose is already cooked, you just don't know it yet.

——————

A couple kids I was training, they got me to thinking. They started tuning me real good … to the bomb-laden van full of Israelis on 9/11 … the ones giving each other high fives in Jersey City. The "Dancing Jew commandos."

I had forgotten about it. A quick glimpse, a short news flash on CNN. A teeny-tiny paragraph in the New York Times … unimportant. Undeserving of a follow up … not with the new iPod being launched … I was all confused inside. I was a perfect American.

Hhhhhmmm … I start thinking some more. I exercise a little gray matter:

How did Peter Bergen score an exclusive interview with Osama Bin Laden in 1997? How did he find the sheikh's little dessert get away? The mobile Ramada Inn made of sheets?

Supposedly the greatest military and intelligence force in the world looking for this guy … there's reason for suspicion … CIA … NSA … satellites doing double overtime circling the planet … drones … spies … Clinton even sending a little care package. A cruise missile love letter from the sky … only thing: nobody home! … Bin Laden and his royal hunting buddies, they got word to skedaddle … Like I said, it pays to know the Bushes.

But this Bergen … no heads up? … how about an "over here!"

No. No. No. No. No … much more convenient to come back with footage of Bin Laden declaring war on the U.S.

Really?

From way over there?

From a cave?

Billions of dollars or no billions of dollars … his team's equipped with dirty sox and Underoose.

Now I start reminiscing … I'm special that way. Putting two and two together.

The lies … there were more than a few fibs.

The weapons of mass destruction? The famous WMD?

Well, maybe an honest mistake … costly! … for sure! … in lives, resources and political good will. But things do get misplaced.

But Private First Class Jessica Lynch? The rescue?

Total Hollywood production!

Assaulting the hospital in night vision … total bullshit!

The Iraqi doctors … with her feet up and feeding her intravenously … they call us … boop, boop, boop … "Come pick up your girl."

Then there's Pat Tillman.

They had a real legit American hero story going for them … with his turning down NLF millions to kill Arabs. For revenge!

First the Taliban killed him … Official story! Front-page news! … sure made all the families who's sons died or came back looking like RoboCop — with their little bionic legs and arms — feel better.

But these damn whistleblowers … snitches … can't anyone keep their trap shut?

Now it's friendly fire! A big case of: ooops!

A second Official Story … he's screaming for his life, begging our armor-trucked machine gunner to hose somebody else down. Someone darker. Muslim preferably.

Fog of war! … it happens … Pat Tillman, Osama Bin Laden … we're lucky no one has shot big boss Obama yet. If anyone can pass for a desert insurgent its him. Toss him a towel, an AK … skip a few shaves … the difference is in the five o'clock shadow. That's all.

But then the autopsy … our beloved science. Facts. Indisputable evidence … they're only anxious to share when it points to Cro-Magnon Man.

… Three shots from close range; to the back of the head … NATO .556 rounds. That's our own bullets.

… Reports of discontent amongst the troops. Specifically: "Tillman's aggressive atheism."

He came out a little too soon! Another one who couldn't leave well enough alone … a few more years? … they would've made him general! Commander-in-Chief! The high tide of secularism isn't receding anytime soon.

You're not going to beat 9/11, though. When it comes to theatrics, these motherfuckers make Shakespeare look like a GoPro-wielding amateur.

I'm not going to spell it out for you. I'm not going to do all your homework … just a few hints … Google is a marvelous Trojan Horse tool. Join me on NSA's watch list.

World Trade Center Building 7… Great place to start! … would've been the tallest building in 30 other states … straight down like an accordion! Into a little neat pile like the other two towers …. poor owner Larry Silverstein. He happened to call out sick that day … to get a pimple popped. His two kids decided to sleep in.

Building 7 and the Towers: only steal-framed buildings to collapse due to fire … historic! … time to call back the scientists … for a little analysis … a little insto presto on how the impossible happened … three times in a single day.

Too bad all that steel was immediately carted off, melted down and sold to China.

And the Pentagon … I get to wondering again … why is there no footage of the plane? … my local 7/11 has better video surveillance than the Pentagon?

Oh wait, there's one video on Youtube … they made a mistake letting that get out! … clearly a missile … level … no more than 10 feet off the ground.

That explains the lawn; the scene of the supposedly jumbo jet crash landing … like the fairway at Pinehurst No. 2 … forget a smoldering trail … not a scratch!

No plane or bodies, either.

Where's NORAD? What happened to radar and the billions we spent with Lockheed Martin?

We can shoot down a Scud but can't find Mohammed Atta cruising the eastern seaboard?

Fuck the boop … boop … boops … and the blip … blip … blips … Look up! Pull over! Wipe the sleepers out of your eyes!

We're all down here … he's the only one up there!

Well, him and Bin Laden's family.

Special privileges … again, the Bushes. They're great chums. Even the birds were ordered to land but not the Bin Laden's … they're flying the coop … definitely don't want to be around when we pin this on their MK-Ultra Manchurian Candidate kid.

Atta must've really had the right stuff … veteran pilots said those planes would've disintegrated at the proposed speeds and altitudes … too bad Al-Qaeda got to him before NASA … he could've crash landed our shuttle on Pluto.

Last but not least: the follow up slur campaign.

Devote Muslims … willing to die for their beliefs … not before taking an all expense paid trip to Vegas! Not without some lap dances!

George Bush was right … Mission Accomplished! … hook, line and sinker … loosen the drag … you can give Americans as much line as you want. They'll run with it. Just don't take their Starbucks away.

❧

Speaking of fat, distracted Americans … Steve, my executive editor, he was getting himself into a pickle on multiple fronts.

For starters, he didn't feel like writing anymore. It was beneath him … He had discovered his specialty. His niche … taking PR girls out to lunch and dinner on daddy Hearst's dime ... and why not? The money had been pouring in.

There were a few reprimands, thought. A couple indiscretions ... one too many unrequited advances on our interns ... he thought anyone could do it. That scooping up Jodi was easy. Those free dinners had gone to his head.

Lucky for him, daddy Hearst likes to settle out of court. He doesn't want anyone peeping his riches, peeking under the bed ... you have no idea what you'd fine under there. Our office was a mini Moulin Rouge. A satellite brothel of misfits and deviants. ... careful bending over for toner at the copy machine!

But Steve's biggest offense: his oversized paycheck!

After 10 years as the No. 2 man, the co-pilot — having successfully navigated the clear, calm skies of the greatest financial windfall in history — Steve was gone.

A little turbulence?

Right out the door!

Decent parachute, though ... a year's pay plus benefits.

We immediately hired a new No. 2 ... Ken Ryan. He liked me ... he noted how prolific I was with copy ... always the hustler ... boxes, roofs, breaking news ... I'm aware I'm in competition to keep food in my mouth.

Ken had a front-row seat for 9/11 ... he witnessed the human water balloons going splat ... permanent mental scar! ... I could hear him through the office wall weeping ... as useful as a limp dick! A broken man.

The one definitive thing he did?

Write an honest editorial about Pergo ... the largest seller and advertiser of the click-clack plastic wood floors I'm always going on about ... boy did he spell out how they betrayed the specialty retailer; their going direct to Home Depot was a big No No.

Didn't take long … one week … Pergo pulled their entire advertising budget.

Just like that: minus $350,000.00

Pergo's CEO made it pretty clear: "Fuck you! I'll never give you bastards a penny."

Swiiiiiiiissshhhhhhhh … there goes Ken! Right out the Hearst window!

He didn't get the same parachute as Steve. He's lucky they let him leave with his shoes.

⚉

It dawned on me that I wasn't exactly on the fast track to success. Far from it.

My solution? My big idea?

Start an amateur-fighting career at 31!

It's amazing what you can fail at if you just try.

I go for the medical exam. The piss test … everything's A-OK but the doctor lets on, makes a little comment… ain't I a little old for a first fight?

I didn't know enough to be concerned … unlike the unsanctioned matches at Fight House, there'll be boxing gloves and headgear. A referee … there would also be a quasi-medical staff. Some Band-Aids and tape. There's a cooler full of ice.

How bad could it be?

They show me to my locker room, the staging area for those fighting out of the blue corner … lots of guys with coaches and teammates working the pads, circling, pummeling with each other to set up throws. Everyone's focused. Everyone has their hands wrapped and taped.

I don't know how to wrap my hands.

A little late, but here comes Louie, one of Master Chan's disciples … he doesn't know how to wrap a fighter's hands either, but he's a legitimate doctor. Well, he works at Rikers Island Prison Hospital anyway.

I'm in luck, though.

Because I'm a nobody with no record and no legit corner I don't have to wait too long … I don't have to see too many guys come back beat up or with the victorious look of the kill still on their face … I paid my New York Athletic Commission fee. I had my license. It was time to go.

It dawns on me it's not a good sign that I'm wearing a T-shirt to cover up my jellyroll. I'm matching useless pounds of fat against pounds of muscle that wants to hurt me.

The announcer calls me in first … I get a standing ovation … I told you already, it's all smiles and jellybeans on the way to the gallows … if they show you their teeth too soon you might flee.

It's too late for second thoughts.

I circle the ring. I've seen enough fights. I know what I'm supposed to do.

Here comes my opponent … Boy is he tall! And muscular! … I can tell because he's not wearing a T-shirt.

We're toe to toe getting instructions … how lucky everyone in the seats are down there. They get to watch.

Back to the corner … a little water … a little pep talk from Louie.

There's the bell!

There's nothing like your first bell … *Ding. Ding* … either you've been there or you haven't.

The guy comes steaming, charging at me. He's trying to end it quick.

I land a solid front kick to his midsection … it bends him over. It backs him up.

It's good for my confidence but he's sticking to his game plan … here he comes again.

I jam his strikes. I land two heavy ones of my own … his power doesn't impress me. I'm not scared anymore.

Now I got him in the corner. Now it's time for me to show him a thing or two.

His hands are up, covering his head … I'm really going to town. Punching with everything I got.

Zero effect!

A pillow fight!

He can take it all night. I might've been boring him.

He slips his arms under my armpits as we clinch.

What's this?

I see the ground rushing up at me.

I didn't bounce.

I was expecting to bounce.

I'm back up. The ref steps between us and then signals to go at it again.

He's trying to use his height, his longer arms … he 's jabbing at me. The old one, two.

I jam him up again. I give him a good crack to the head … he's back in the corner.

Here I go again with my ineffectual flurries … is he napping? … he doesn't flinch … he just covers up and takes it.

Now here he goes again with his under-the-armpits routine … the up, up and away … an upside-down blur of multi-colored ropes with people cheering behind them … the ceiling lights … his bare legs … another big *CRASH!*!!!

That one fucking hurt!

The air leaves my body. My shoulder. My ribs.

I'm a little wobbly inside. I could throw up if I wanted to.

I hear a second bell. There's nothing like the second bell when things aren't going well.

Back in my corner, Louie thinks I'm doing great. He's all pumped up. He slaps my fucking head ... it took a lot not to punch him ... he doesn't get it ... I'm exhausted ... I can't fight anymore. One more drop on my head and it's going to take more than all the king's horses and all the king's men.

Fuck, there's the bell again.

I got to go back out.

It would soon be clear I couldn't win. That I would soon forget what it's like to be a winner.

CHAPTER 16:

ROUND AND ROUND AFTER MANY ROUNDS

"To be nobody but yourself in a world which is doing its best, night and day, to make you everybody else means to fight the hardest battle which any human being can fight; and never stop fighting." — E.E. Cummings

Alone.

Alone flying south at 35,000 feet.

Alone clutching my seat through turbulence, nonchalantly raising the window shade to sneak a peek with each terrifying rattle. Trying to will the craft into smooth air.

Alone surrounded by clapping Puerto Ricans as we touch down safely in Aguadilla. It's like we're surprised to be alive. We've cheated death.

Alone watching everyone else's luggage go round and round and round the carousel.

Alone dragging my board bag to Budget's rental counter ... the bastards at Enterprise still have me black balled.

Outside: sweet, pungent, early-morning tropical dew … the moon and stars fight a losing battle against the rising sun. Palm trees. Foreign voices. Calm. Quiet … New York seems a million miles away. Flamboyan trees drizzle me with their flaming red pedals.

Alone standing on the shores of Wilderness, realizing it's way too big … too much water moving. Large peaks breaking way outside but sweeping towards Aguada like a raging river. Water spilling over into the parking lot.

Climbing the winding hills of Rincon, alone.

Lush tropical scenery pouring through the windows, alone.

Grown men, peasants, standing outside the bakery already drunk together but alone … alone in their poverty. Alone in their quiet struggles. Alone with their tranquility.

I wasn't alone when I got to Marias!

One hundred people already in the water! More about to jump in!

Cars, pickup trucks, Volkswagen buses, bikes, mopeds, vans … strewn about everywhere!

Vehicles spilling over from the parking lot into fields, onto mounds, under trees, into ditches, up embankments … I'll need a metal detector to find my way back through these tall bushes.

The best part about parking in the boondocks? Backing into virgin jungle for natural camouflage? … not the ticks and scrapes! … but maybe no one will smash my window.

I give myself 50/50 odds.

Anyway, I have a plan … I'm going to take out my antique Hansen 50/50 longboard. The one with the bolted skeg.

Paddle. Paddle. Paddle … I either timed it right or got lucky … either way, I'm out. I'm a long way from freezing in New York.

It's like a dream.

All the shiny and rusty metal piled up on shore … the broken windows, beer bottles and people … obscured from the lineup by a landscape rising dramatically with lush peaks and jagged valleys. A blending of solitude and the mechanical advancements of man.

Blue powerful water. Green majestic peaks.

Here's my chance! A good one! Maybe seven feet tall … the wave … paddle. paddle. paddle … I can already taste it. I can see myself pulling in, waving to all the girlies.

Nope. A dud … at least that's what I tell myself … "nobody could've caught it" … some waves just flatten out, take a funny bounce.

Not the one behind it!

Twice as big!

Huge!

Taller than my landlord's house.

… the lip is way up there! Worse still, it's coming down on me.

Hold the autographs!

I take back my make-believe gesture to the girlies … Now I hope no one's looking. Now I'm trying to figure out what to do.

Rule No. 1: hold my breath! … goes without saying. These Boriqua hotties ain't gonna swim to my rescue. They're not going to play Bay Watch and give me CPR, a little mouth-to-mouth resuscitation.

To throw the board or not to throw the board … that's the question now!

Tossing the board and swimming to the bottom is appealing; it has its advantages.

You certainly don't want to cling to a 10-foot board and take the full impact bobbing on the surface … you want to separate yourself from what will inevitably become a projectile … you want to get deep; under the turbulence.

Who knows, maybe you'll get spared and pop right up on the other side … maybe the board will tug you a bit. A little yank on the leg … that's what the leash is for, isn't it?

That's the theory.

What often happens is the leash breaks right away. Your board goes bouncing helter-skelter like a cannonball at everyone behind you … it's a great way to make friends!

What do I do?

I cling to my scud missile!

I try to submerge myself and my cannonball as best I can. I try to recreate Waterloo in 15-feet of water.

There's a trick to it, a method: Turtle Rolling … you flip the board over, point it towards the incoming crashing wave and hold on from below. You anchor yourself to nothing and hope for the best.

Miraculously, it worked. Me and the board were still there, together … just a little beating. A little tossing around. Barely worth a mention.

I flip the board back over and hop on.

Now the adrenaline is going.

The waves don't wait for you. They keep coming.

What's this? More turbulence? And at the surface?

Something isn't right. I've ridden this jalopy enough. It's like my old Cadillac … *smooth!* … just don't try to turn it too tight … but it's faltering.

I flip it over … Frontsies. Backsies … everyone must be getting a real kick out of me. Like I'm flipping pancakes at 7:00a.m. in eight-foot surf.

Completely buckled! A three-foot swath of fiberglass flapping like a flag … ooh, look! … lucky me! … it even cut me open … now I got some fiberglass embedded in my shin.

Well, obviously it's time to go in … not my best session … or longest.

Wait, here comes another one.

It's my chance.

I can redeem myself.

Damaged board or no damaged board.

I stroke into it … it's starting to get away from me, too, but my frustration propels me further … I'm in. I will it … I'm up, careful to keep the floppy nose out of the water as I take the drop.

I make my bottom turn.

Oh wait … there's one … no, two … no … three, four, five, six and even seven other surfers in my way.

I have to straighten out … the parties over … I'm pointed directly to shore.

That's precisely when the front three feet of the board snap off and smack me across the kneecaps.

Who has time for pain? … I don't want to be the polluting gringo. My airplane was still refueling. My rental car hadn't had time to overheat and melt the surf wax allover the glove compartment.

I find the fucking missile … it hadn't gone too far … from the nose to my kneecaps to bobbing right beside me … How thoughtful! How considerate!

I tuck the splintered nose under my chest — more fiberglass wounds — and paddle half a board in … I'm careful to stub my toes once or twice on the shoreline rocks; gather a couple sea urchin spines for good luck. It'll give me something to do at the hotel. A little science project. A little game of Operation without the batteries and annoying buzzer … good thing I brought tweezers.

I'm bugging out on the balcony of the Ocean Front Hotel, enjoying the Sour Diesel I smuggled in the hollow of my deodorant.

The surf was still breaking way out in front of Punto Jacinto, the lagoon point break at Playa Jobos ... I could see it from where I was. Sprawled out on a lounge chair, feeling the sun and my little shards of fiberglass swaying in the breeze.

An athletic bikini-clad blonde ... busty but with a small, tight waist ... definitely not shy! She's got her beach towel draped over her forearm ... the other hand's removing her sunglasses. She's shaking her hair out in the breeze.

She's not young ... but definitely proud of herself. She's into what she's got.

Here comes her chubby husband. He doesn't make it all the way out to the balcony. He's squeezed, pinched between the hallway's tight corridor ... trapped with a board bag and suitcase. He's struggling with the weight ... his and the gear.

Wait ... what's this?

It's mommy's little mini-me ... surfer Barbie with the bleach-blonde hair. Same shape as mom, only smaller, tighter, more youthful and supple.

Before I can completely perv out, here comes someone else scuttering down the hallway ... it's turning into a real traffic jam ... Tommy Bahama's never going to get out. He and his board bag, luggage and Hawaiian shirt ... stuck for life.

It's another hottie ... a young brunette ... an early twenties Gothie in black eye makeup, bikini and knee-high boots.

The day was getting more interesting by the moment ... those little urchin spikes in my foot? I wasn't thinking about them.

The Aryan Surf Federation finally cleared out. It's just me and Elvira ... I can tell she doesn't surf. It certainly doesn't matter.

She's got a little secret for me.

She leans in close. She really wants to share … "I can smell the weed on you."

It's times like this I've learned to be generous.

We're back in my room. It's right there. The last room at the end of the hall, right before the balcony.

Elvira's yapping about her boyfriend while I'm rolling a joint. We're sitting on my bed. Me, her, her bikini and boots … he's downstairs checking in … he's fumbling with all his D.J. equipment … apparently, he's too cheap to spring for a taxi … they hitchhiked down the mountain.

Obviously, this all bothers me … being duped out of a joint … his having the girl and getting away without a rental car.

To make matters worse, she convinces me to bring the joint down to his room. He's on the first floor … a recent extension … smaller! Definitely a smaller room!

He tells me how he brings his D.J. equipment everywhere. Won't travel without it! He makes it clear! The two won't part!

I'm definitely more interested in his girlfriend. And changing the horrible music … he's converted his tiny bungalow into a studio. He's wired for sound.

I make sure to hit my joint deeply and multiple times when it comes back around. Fuck the "puff, puff, pass" when it's your own weed.

Knowing Elvira's slipped through my hands I think about cutting out … taking my joint to Surfers Beach … a few waves … something to possess momentarily. Something to call my own.

"Do you want some chocolate-covered mushrooms?"

A large Zip Lock Bag emerges from a hidden speaker compartment. It's dangling in front of my face.

A mix of excitement and concern rushes over me.

Tripping?

In Puerto Rico?

While surfing? And driving?

Alone?

He drops three chocolate balls in my hand and I plop three choc-olate balls down my throat.

By the time I get to Surfers Beach and paddle out I'm getting the free medical exam … X-Ray vision! … there's my ulna and radius … there's all my carpals, metacarpals and all three kind of phalanges. The surf is crystalline. I'm leaving a wake of fluttering diamonds.

I had lost touch with the divine … so busy and worried about deadlines, making ends meat to pay rent. So careful about everything! … you can't afford slip-ups when you're on your own.

I forgot what it was like to expect magic. I had forgotten to create futures with my mind for time to catch up to.

I'm right back to it … same gig. Standing in the ring chubby wearing a T-shirt.

I learned. I wised up … I did the whole running on the beach thing to prepare. I had no excuse not to. It was right there … the grey, cold, compact New York shoreline.

It wasn't wise, though, to taunt the promoter on a public Internet forum; or to generally sign up for the New Jersey San Da World Championships. But given that I did so poorly the last time, I figured a tournament format would give me more chances … Chances for what, I hadn't the faintest idea. Certainly not winning … I told you. Those days were over.

I drew Stephan Cloud, a professional Mixed Martial Artist moon-lighting as an amateur San Da fighter. A hobbyist kick boxer … he wasn't wearing a T-shirt.

His game plan was simple, unflawed and perfectly executed … come in, beat the hell out of me and then back off … Dance a bit. Circle. Gesture to the crowd.

Twice he came in a little too hard and lingered a little too long.

The ref stopped the clock when I got back to my feet the second time … that's the last thing I wanted. The seconds couldn't tick tock fast enough.

With his powdered blue latex glove he grabs the base of my nose and says, "Don't blow out. Hold your breath."

He gives it a good tug. A nice jerk … a glob of my blood pours out into his towel.

He's taking his time. He thinks he's helping with the stall tactics … He wants me to recover.

"It's broken. Do you still want to fight?"

What am I supposed to say?

I know what I wanted to say.

It didn't really matter. I was utterly defeated but we'd go through the motions anyway.

Cloud comes right for me.

I land a couple kicks. For a second I made him think twice … He must've tired a bit beating on me.

He goes for the finish … total disregard for me and my safety! … a huge, professionally-powered roundhouse kick to the head!!! My head!!!

I don't try to back away. On the contrary, I step in. I keep compact … I had a nice little wedging structure going for myself.

I catch him just right!

He's off his feet!

Most everyone probably thought he slipped … most likely on my blood.

Did the referee see it? Did he appreciate the technique?

Either way, now Cloud's pissed. Now he's precise … one, two, three … Whack! Whack! Whack!

I'm down! Again!

They stop it after three … for everyone's sake. Otherwise it could get boring.

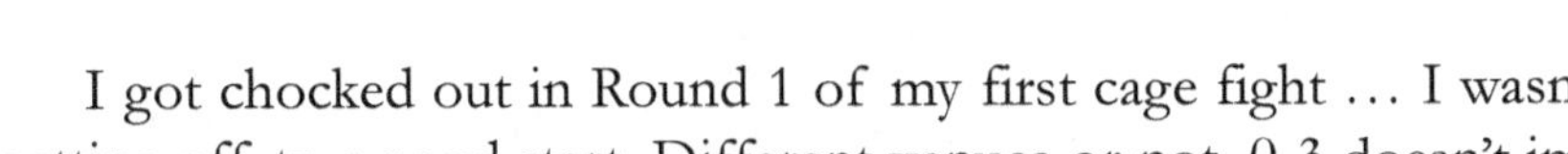

I got chocked out in Round 1 of my first cage fight … I wasn't getting off to a good start. Different venues or not, 0-3 doesn't impress anyone.

It started off well enough, with me closing the distance, getting the better of the exchanges. I landed a coco tasso or two … and then … then they pulled a little hocus pocus. A little abracadabra … they pulled out the jiu-jitsu.

These bastards have a way of latching onto your leg, your arm, your head. You think you can punch your way out but you can't … they cramp your style … they want to crash into you … a little bundle on the floor? … they couldn't be happier!

I wasn't the only one being dropped.

Floor sales? … not what they used to be!

Turns out the only thing that could impede the largest economic growth in history was the bill … and a couple global invasions. Little in-between wars.

I'm covering a Shaw Industries convention. Warren Buffet just bought the company, fired the founder and CEO and is about to give a speech … this should be interesting; informative.

Despite declining sales, he's 100 percent optimistic about the overall flooring industry, particularly for Shaw!

Wait, he's got more to say … he didn't come all this way for nothing. He's philosophizing … he's not too dissimilar from the rest of us … he eats hamburgers, drinks Coke and sleeps in a regular bed in a regular-sized house.

I look around at the stadium seating, this huge auditorium filled with the nation's largest flooring dealers … They believe him! They're buying this bullshit … they've fallen for the smile and ice cream cone routine. Him with all the "I and the other billionaires should pay more taxes."

Why shouldn't they fall for it?

These saps, dancing on millions of their own, they'll believe anything.

So what if Buffet is 100 percent tax exempt!

That's what these start-up millionaires are for. To carry the burden … someone's got to pay.

I'm starting to get over it. Over pretty much everything in general.

Floor Covering Weekly has me flying to Orlando every other week … five conventions in two months and no Mickey Mouse.

My friends back in Long Beach? The mediocre Satanists with the basement rock band … they won't let me on the mic … they prefer to make a hell of a racket without lyrics … I have to say, it insults me. That they never ask.

The real kicker; the turning point: standing for the bus at 6:00 a.m. in the dark … my feet buried in a foot of snow. My socks soaking wet. My nose raw from wiping away the dripping snot.

Fuck this!!!!!

It dawns on me there's hardly any surf in Long Beach … all this sand and all these jetties and no waves. And when there is a little bump on the ocean … head-to-toe in rubber. A human 5mm condom.

My real friends are dead. My family, while in New Jersey, might as well be on the moon … I'm going in circles … working, training, losing fights. Smoking weed with the neighbors.

The girls that I could get, I didn't want to keep. The ones I wanted to keep didn't want to stay. And the ones that remained weren't interested.

Two hours later I get to the office. I'm stewing in my wet socks … I'm tired of punching in codes to get through the door and to take a shit. I'm sick of singing happy birthday, fire drills, baby showers … the office is worse than prison! I'd take solitary any day! … It's not the work. It's the people!

"Sandy. I want to work from home."

He considers it. The eyes go to the ceiling for a second, shift to the right and to the left. It's not an unprecedented request. We have outside writers in Dalton, Corpus Christi and San Diego.

"Well, you'll lose your 401(k)."

It labored me not to laugh. The idea that I could have enough money left over at the end of the month for investing.

"And your health benefits … You'll lose them. You won't be an employee anymore. You'll be on a monthly retainer."

I liked the sound of that!

A samurai for hire! … I was already practically working for sacks of rice.

Then I snuck it in … "and I want to move to Puerto Rico."

He's immediately concerned about travel, that it would cost too much getting back and forth. Him and his budget … and that I would fall off the map, fuck everything up surfing the day away … he definitely knew who he was dealing with.

But I furnish printouts from JetBlue and Expedia. I came prepared … it's actually cheaper to get to Orlando and Las Vegas from Puerto Rico!

That intrigues him! With print advertising going the way of the Dodo, every penny counts.

Of course, he lets me know he's going out of his way, making an exception. He's doing me a favor … he also warns about being a private contractor, having to file a 1040 and keeping enough aside to pay the taxman.

I wasn't concerned about my retirement or dental. I wasn't worrying about the IRS … this wasn't a strategic retreat. It was desertion.

Crazies flying planes into buildings.

Grammar School shootings

High School shootings.

University shootings.

Mall shootings.

Grocery store shootings of congresswomen.

Sniper fire in D.C.

Moving to Puerto Rico is more affordable than maintaining a Kevlar wardrobe … it was time to change theaters. Put a little space between me and the center of the bullseye.

CHAPTER 17:

——— ⌇ ———

EXCELLING IN EXILE

"I have to run like a fugitive to save the life I live. I'm gonna be iron like a lion in Zion." — *Bob Marley*

Following your heart; it's not something for the masses. They need to know the how and why about a thing. They need to be able to weight it so they can calculate, contrive, plot and plan. They won't do a thing unless there're additional dollar signs.

My father, he couldn't understand how I could just mail a check to Puerto Rico for an apartment sight unseen; pack up what little I had and ship it by container to an unknown address.

Of course, there were also the haters. The ones who wanted to make light of my heroics ... "It's still the U.S.," they said.

Maybe so. Debatable.

What was not up for debate was my phone line ... Absolutely not! Was not going to happen! ... something about no room and switchboards and not going out of the way for a gringo.

163

"But, but, my neighbors have a landline. The cable goes right past my place. Can't we tap it?"

Nope!

Again, it's not a matter of tapping … no vacancy on the switchboard! … Tu hablas Ingles gringo?

You know who wasn't interested in conversing in English? … the whole lineup at Playa Jobos!

I got a special greeting.

Local competitor Wilfredo Deliz, AKA Control … boy did they name him right. He and his buddies ushered me off … those weren't pom-poms swinging in my face.

They maintain a nice little arsenal stashed around that dilapidated fishing skiff. Just for this sort of occasion: loud-mouthed gringos.

When I tell you Jobos is locked down I'm not kidding!

Be careful!

You'd do best not to go … that's what Playa Middles was made for.

⚬⚬⚬

Solitude! Real solitude! … not this phoney baloney "I'm turning off my phone" or "shutting down my computer" bullshit.

No landline!

No cell phone signal or Internet service!

Just me and a handful of neighbors on a dead-end street … more cows than people wedged between the tropical sea and a single-lane road at the foot of a cliff that pins us here.

I catch the old lady next door going through my garbage every morning. She doesn't expect me up so early. We pretend we don't notice each other … our own little game of peek-a-boo … What she's looking for? Your guess is as good as mine.

I watch working-aged men come and tear down the aluminum, copper … they're tearing down that home cinderblock by cinderblock. They've stolen everything … you can't take a long leave of absence around here. I learned that already. Don't leave your car parked in the same spot too long, either. People might get ideas. That you're not coming back … first your tires. You'll find your car sitting on those "borrowed" cinderblocks. You're now AutoZone … your windshield wipers, doors, radio, steering wheel, battery. Bit by bit carted off for better use. Not-for-you use.

I got chased out of Jobos again. This time by a bigger crowd with a larger assortment of weapons … now I get the point.

My only friends are teenage up-and-coming pro surfers. They like to visit, borrow my bong … it amuses them that I fill it with ice. A little trick I brought with me from the north.

They tell me how much danger I'm in. That I should move to Rincon with the other gringos … they have been warned, too: standing next to me is not safe! These guys are not very accurate! They don't spring for the laser sights and telescopic scopes.

I quit skateboarding the quarter mile to the gas station for coffee … I've been run off the road twice. Intentionally. Full on try-to-kill-me swerves … with me diving for the bushes … it gets so that I have to sneak around. Take a peek here and there … Is so and so surfing? … no? … perfect! I jump in to catch a few waves … I develop a little system. I sit off to the side. Put on an air of amazement. That these guys are really impressing me … soon as a good one comes through: let them all paddle for it! Curse each other! Bump rails! Drop in on each other! … five guys go at once … then I take the one behind it … all to my self … just me and the dirty looks.

It's not rare for people to throw or ditch their boards, just to sabotage my wave … maybe they'll get lucky and smash my shin or kneecap … the lineup is definitely divided: Those that absolutely, unquestionably hate my presence. They're not shy about it … and the ones that like or tolerate me but can't say so.

No one expects me to stick around too long. Not long enough to ostracize themselves as a race trader.

I try to advertise the last name … Piña! … P-I-Ñ -A … it doesn't matter. Me no speaky Spanish.

I'm not the only gringo in the area; I'm just the only one that doesn't live on Ramey Base.

Coast Guard, Border Patrol, Army, Air Force, Navy… for a deactivated base: super packed!

B-52s, Predator drones, U2 spy planes.

Gigantic C-17 Army transport vehicles; unmarked Black Hawk helicopters … there's definitely some hanky panky going on.

Then there's the restricted "solar observatory" … sitting right there above us on the cliff. Above me and my neighbors and the cows … part of a local network … with the two golf-ball-shaped radar domes … the H.A.A.R.P. antenna array.

They're cooking up the ionosphere real good! The clouds come in every shape but normal. They fan out like fish scales or concentric circles. Often with a rainbow lining.

All this gear and I can't maintain an Internet connection; the key to my work-from-home agreement. The office wants to see me logged on constantly … underwear or no underwear … that's my business. But always available via Instant Messenger.

I'm at Choice Cable three, four times a week … it's like waiting at a doctor's office. Bring a book! If you get there around 10 a.m. pack a lunch! You'll need it.

Thirteen radar dishes on their property — I've counted — and no fucking signal! It's beyond me.

"Hola. Buenas dia." … that's me at Choice Cable. They know me. We've developed a relationship.

The running joke is that there's no competition. It's Choice Cable or dominos. That's the choice.

I go through a modem a week. I wonder what they think I'm doing with the fucking things.

When they want to stop by and wiggle a couple wires; when they think that might help, I try to provide an address for a location without one in Spanglish:

"Yo este en kilometer uno, hector quatro…. on the side of Calle 466."

That's as close as I can zero you in. After that you'll have to follow me. It's not far. But good luck finding it on your own.

I know the office back home thinks I'm on a permanent vacation.

They think I'm swaying under palm trees in a hammock with a margarita ... there's no hammock or margarita ... I have to hightail it to the beach to get cell reception. I'm stretching the phone out this way. I'm stretching the phone out that way. My own little yoga routine ... I'd wear a tinfoil hat except I'm still making up for botched first impressions.

❧

My neighbor Loncho stops me in the middle of the street; he's shirtless, barefoot and wearing stained, torn jeans held in place by rope. He wants to show me something important. He wants my opinion.

I'm intrigued … he tells me to wait while he runs back inside the house. He and his wife, well, they're not technically married, but they're descended from pirates. Both of them. To see them, to know them … no question about it.

From time to time Loncho works on vacation rental properties. He can fix anything. He's concocted his own built-in swimming pool … Puerto Rican detail all the way! … pipes here and there, rough corners, duct tape. But functional! And better than you or I could do! And on a strict budget!

He hurries back out. Boy does he really want to show me something … he jams a warm photo into my hands. Apparently, the pirates have updated to digital printing.

"Uh-huh. Uh-huh." I'm not sure how to react.

Is this art?

It's a picture of the cliff up the block … with some sporadic cloud cover.

He turns me, faces me in the proper direction. He wants to give me some perspective … he's pointing. He's highlighting a blotch in his Puerto Rican Peter Lik.

"Yeah?"

He's getting aggravated … he zeroes me in again on the watermark. Then he's pointing to the sky. He's zigzagging his finger back and forth.

Now I understand what he's getting at.

"A UFO? You think this is from outer space?"

He's disappointed. He thinks his photo fell on deaf ears.

Actually, he came to the right guy. I'm practically on Pluto already … it was simply a matter of poor timing. I had just gotten off the phone with my skeptical brother. He and his scientific method.

"That could be a raindrop or something on the lens" … now I'm shitting on *his* parade. Insinuating he's some hick. A Puerto Rican hillbilly.

But I'm the one who's ignorant. A real ignoramus … like I said, they're not going out of the way to dispel rumors about the base … the underground missile silos, the secret take offs and landings … they have their own little Area 51 down in Lajas and Parguera … flying discs, orbs of light. Bring some pinchos with your binoculars.

I wasn't quite catching on yet, though. I still sort of believed CNN … Not the weapons of mass destruction nonsense. Or the whole thing about "Mission Accomplished" … not in our lifetime … but that Merrill Lynch wrote off $8.4 billion in bad mortgages. And that it would be O.K.

What's the worst that could happen?

Surely Merrill Lynch isn't going away … worst-case scenario some Japanese corporation will snatch it up, add the financial icon to their No-Longer-American portfolio.

I smelled opportunity!

I set up a TD Ameritrade account … with $400-a-month rent — all inclusive — I'm able to stash away a few thousand dollars.

I buy the Jim Cramer books. I start buying MER in small blocks. First at $78 a share, down from its original $98 … boy am I getting a real bargain … then it hits the $60s … whooo yooo!!! Now I'm really getting my money's worth!

I'm an expert. A genius. I tell the bum who crashes at my neighbor's, the ones who live in San Juan and run a school for the well-to-do kids, who visit on the weekends … "You have to save. Invest" … "You can't keep mooching your whole life" … "There's only so much semi-precious metal to swipe off the block" … "Recycled aluminum can only take you so far."

Then MER goes to $50 … Jim Cramer warned me. He made it clear: Don't panic!

Then MER goes to $40 … What does Warren Buffet say? Be greedy when others are fearful?

Well, everyone's shitting their pants … CNN says everyone's mortgage, their home's value … kapoot! Now you see it, now you don't wealth.

Good thing I don't have a 401(k). Everyone got had pretty good. The joke was on us … turns out you can't really buy a home without a job or no money down … you just borrowed it for a bit. Now they're taking it back.

This George Bush … he inspires me to start learning Chinese. There's talk of nationalizing the banks … to save them.

What happened to all this free market talk? What about the "communism-is-the-devil" racket? Laissez faire?

Wow. A whole bunch of people died for nothing fighting the commies … I'm not going to hit you over the head with it. There's a reason they call it a Depression. You're probably better off not knowing. Comfortably numb. Ignorance is bliss. Opium for the masses. You get the picture … not only are they not trying to help you … 100 percent scheming to take your money! And for you to tote the bill!

I wake up one morning … am I dreaming? … do I have sleepers in my eyes?

Where did my precious MER go?

Gone! No longer exists! The letters M-E-R now replaced with B-A-C. Now I'm a Bank of America shareholder … where and when was the meeting? Why was I not invited? And why did we settle for such a low price? … what started out at $98 a share reduced to $29 … I'm not going to attract any clientele with a return like that.

These fuckers.

Me and my high school friends though we were slick skipping out on the bill at Pizza Hut … Child's play! Amateurish! … these motherfuckers slip us a bill for $431 billion! … the Troubled Asset Relief Program (TARP) … no shit? … I've had troubled assets my entire life. How about no assets!

Now I see what they're doing; what they're up to.

Of course, it's too late. I can only watch BAC drop to $2.53 and go along for the ride … now I have to root that we get Osama Bin Laden. That we drop a little care package on his lap; or send in a mysterious whirlybird packed with Navy Seals.

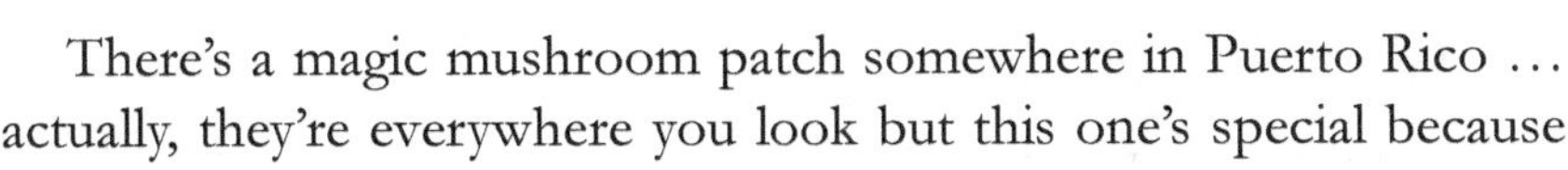

There's a magic mushroom patch somewhere in Puerto Rico ... actually, they're everywhere you look but this one's special because it's the one I'm familiar with.

There I go under the barbed wire fence. The only dangers are fresh heaps of cow shit, two or three bulls with baseball-bat-length horns and the police, which for some reason or another make frequent passes but never stop ... I'm making believe that I need to stand in the middle of this pasture to get better cell phone service, the phone held to my ear like a moron. Or I have my camera out ... "Oh me? I'm just taking pictures."

Of what, you ask?

Would you believe cows?

Yes, I'm taking pictures of these lovely Puerto Rican cows ... or mushrooms. I'm doing field research. Don't ask me for what university or affiliation ... strictly an amateur. A backyard botanist.

And then there's the Italian defense.

"Oh, I heard this is the place to get mushrooms. I'm making the sickest pasta sauce tonight."

The police just pass. All worried over nothing and there they go ... zooooom.

And the bulls? The bulls are too cool in the shade to bother about me on this hot day.

Todo bien. Puerto Rico lo hace major ... Verdad!

[A CONVERSATION THAT CAN ARISE ANGER JUST AS EASILY AS THE ENLIGHTNEMENT OF CAUSE AND EFFECT]

"I got my ex-girlfriend pregnant."

What you going to do?

"I got to find a job."

Did you check at that construction site up the block?

"Nah, they only want Dominicans."

How about Villa Montana?

"No. They won't hire me either."

Well, you're an educated man. Why don't you go back to school, finish your degree?

"I can't."

Why not?

"Because I used my student loan to travel and didn't pay it back."

Where'd you go?

"Costa Rica and Panama."

Are they after you?

"Who?"

The loan officers? The banks?

"Fuck them. They ain't getting anything."

Man. That's rough. I'll keep my ears open for ya.

[I offered Omar one of the few Coronas I was saving for when I had female company.]

"Hey, I'm going to go pick up a bag. Do you want to come along?"

Nah, I can't. I got some work to do and I'm giving it a rest ... at least for a while.

"That gringo that was staying next to you ... did he leave?"

Yeah. Why?

"Fucking guy made a big deal about the count last time. Not only did he come with me, but I let him pick which bag he wanted."

Guys like that give us gringos a bad name.

"Everybody thinks he was a cop."

You guys think we're all cops ... if half of us were cops I might be able to surf without getting jumped.

"It's because the FBI is fucked up. They shot that old man who was a part of the Left movement."

They just went in and shot him?

"Yeah."

They just assassinated him?

"Yeah."

I'm no fan of the government or police but that sounds a little fishy.

"You don't know how it is here. They do it all the time."

The paper said the old man was stockpiling weapons in the mountains.

"Yeah, but these gringos ... they all come down, buy up all the land and now things are getting so expensive."

Hey man, I understand. I've seen the changes, too. But nobody is forcing anybody to sell anything.

"That's not true. You know that farm on the way to Middles? Some guy shot the owner and took it over?"

What?

"Just like that."

A gringo did that?

"Yup."

I'm sorry. I don't buy it ... Nobody did anything?

"Nope."

But if you know, the police and FBI has to know.

"I'm telling you. They're all corrupt. That condo project on the beach ... it's not zoned for that. Its protected land ... the only reason it went through is because the mayor got a penthouse suite out of the deal."

It's like that everywhere, man.

"I'm telling you; they're going to burn that place down."

And they'll wind up in jail and the owner will get the insurance money. That's not the way to do things ... you have to fight it before it's built. Before money's been exchanged.

"I'm telling you, there's going to be a revolution."

I could see it happening. There's definitely enough anti-gringo sentiment.

"They're just using us. They test their chemicals on us!"

Where?

"Right here. I'm telling you."

Is that what caused Chupacabra?

"No. Chupacabra is from space."

<hr>

They wanted to know if I'd pass my test.

"Yeah. Sure. I stopped smoking three months ago."

Silly me ... they were curious if I was cheating; if I was going to register positive for steroids. They could care less about my icy bong hits and magical mushrooms ... it was assumed I was a space cadet. No one in their right mind would take this fight: a gringo in a cage against a local ... they wouldn't match me with the weakest contender. And they certainly wouldn't fly in some non-partisan Yankee referees.

It didn't bolster my confidence when the promoter offered to piss for me ... if needed, he was willing to do it. He didn't want me to worry.

I shouldn't have been surprised ... A year or two before, I survived three rounds to lose a close decision to another local. At least that's what they told me; that it was close.

My friend and training partner Ivan, the reformed gangster who introduced me to my coach ... he stops by. To check up and to critique ... before a fight you have to hear what you should do. Then afterwards, if you loose, you have to hear about what you should've done.

I tell him I'm a little punch drunk. To hold off on any arithmetic.

He doesn't doubt it. He mentions the other guy's gorilla arms ... that he's been monitoring his progress; selling him juice for over a year... a walking billboard! His best customer!

But that's the past.

Now I'm wondering why my opponent isn't packed in this car like a sardine with me and two other young fighters ... The promoter and his partner are escorting us to a piss test that doesn't matter. We're picking up paperwork and a $15 stamp for the license.

I felt great the night of the fight until I saw one of the kids who pissed with me in the cage. He couldn't have weighed more than 140 pounds soaking wet ... he would've licked me ... the way he danced, toyed with his opponent ... ducking, bobbing, weaving. A solid head kick and then *whack!, whack!* ... two to the body ... *crack!* One to the head.

I couldn't watch anymore. I'm back in the locker room ... by gauging the roar of the crowd I could tell what's happening. Soon it would be my turn ... the second to last fight ... watching a local beat a gringo ranked second only to two pro heavyweights flown in from the states.

I discovered that it was a pro event when I got there. The license should have tipped me off but there really wasn't anything I could do … I was there. My hands were taped … To the people in the audience the difference between amateur and professional wouldn't matter. I would be a coward. And they would be right … so I was off to fight.

After the first few exchanges I realize I'm taking damage.

The one shot I'm able to land is heavy and to the center of his face … It rocks him. Backs him up a bit. But I'm too shell shocked to follow up.

Being a professional, he brushes it off. He renews his relentless attack. He keeps firing. I keep blocking. My forearms and shins are taking a beating. I have too many chinks in my armor. I'm soft … I hadn't been fighting enough to callus my body and mind.

I take a desperate dive at his legs and get lucky. I get him down. I have him pinned against the fence when the pyrotechnics go off … a blast of thick white smoke right into my face!

I got Lee Harvey Oswalded!

I have the Zapruder film!

Right then and there I quit. I'm forever done with sport fighting.

I don't resist the triangle choke. I tap while I can still breath, the blood is still flowing to my brain.

I could've stacked him; stepped over his head like I've done countless times in training and tournaments. I could've elbowed him right in his jaw. But now I sound like a fan.

———⌇⌇———

Sooner or later the surf comes up. Not little hot-dog flashy waves, but really up … 12- to 15 feet, with 17- to 20-foot sets.

Now I'm not getting the stink eye.

… lots of locals diverting their gaze.

They don't want to see me seeing them leaving the parking lot.

Forget parking … not even slowing to take a good look at the three-story waves pealing perfectly. They're making U-turns … their dry boards strapped to the roof. The road's too bumpy, too intimate and narrow for their dry hair to go unnoticed.

The waves frighten me. But there they are … perfect!

It's not unlike what drove me into the ring and cage. What leads me to think I could feed myself with words … ability and desire. Though I know my desire outweighs my ability.

Careful!

Super careful!

With a lot of prayers!

I jump in 40 yards further down the point from where everyone usually paddles out.

There's not much to think about. Waves are breaking in the channel where they shouldn't be … I'll either make it out clean or get caught and washed all the way down to Wishing Wells.

I focus on my breathing as I paddle … nice and calm. Again, there's no rush. I'll either make it or not, but I'll need all my energy, air and wits if one of those beasts break in front of me.

It doesn't matter Merrill Lynch never told me it got suckered into buying subprime mortgages. Or that Bank of America colluded with JP Morgan, Citibank, HSB — all the banks — to manipulate derivatives.

It doesn't matter that most Americans are unaware of Operation Northwoods: declassified plans to stage terrorist attacks and blame Castro … they weren't supposed to know.

They're not supposed to know about Jack Parsons and the crater named after him on the dark side of the moon. The satanic roots of his Jet Propulsion Laboratory. And Aleister Crowley … they're not supposed to wonder why there's a District of Columbia, Columbia Pictures, Columbia University, a Space Shuttle Columbia and the Columbia Broadcasting System … they're not supposed to recognize the same deity. The one perched up on Ellis Island … or that CBS' all-seeing-eye logo is the same as the one on the dollar bill. Or that the GOP inverted the stars on its logo. It's all right there in front of us.

But we're not supposed to know. Or care … we're supposed to work and pay our taxes. We're supposed to be comfortable. We're supposed to root for the local team. Or better yet, the winning team.

We're supposed to be accepting. Of everything! To disagree is to discriminate!

To believe in God is to be a fool! Definitely not the winning team! At least not yet!

First, we have to genetically alter everything! All of our food … and eventually ourselves.

The last generation of humans!

Post human is where it's at!

They're creating a new heaven for us. Weather Modification Incorporated … you're not supposed to know about that either …. Perfectly legal! These crisscrossed chemical trails in the sky…. pay no attention to the chessboard overhead. Or that all of your neighbors are autistic. Sniveling is the way to be.

Who's doing this to us? Who's flipping all the stars upside down?

I make it out … there's a few of us out. We're all focused on the waves blocking out the horizon … we're not White, Hispanic, rich or poor. We're the ones who made it out.

PART IV:

DOUBLING DOWN ON THE MATERIAL WORLD

CHAPTER 18:

—❦—

BLINDSIDED BY LOVE AND MADNESS

"We've no use for intellectuals in this outfit. What we need are chimpanzees. Let me give you a word of advice: never say a word to us about being intelligent. We will think for you, my friend. Don't forget it." — *Louis-Ferdinand Celine*

The hypocrisy … it didn't escape me. Like everyone else I simply chose to ignore it.

Working for Hearst and my little fascination with weed … easily reconcilable: I needed to put food in my mouth.

That William Randolph Hearst, though; he certainly did all he could to demonize cannabis … if you invested his mega-millions in forests you would too! Trees for everything!

Forget cannabis' superior yield … Completely lobby against it!

Make it illegal!

… and definitely blame the blacks and Mexicans.

M-A-R-I-J-U-A-N-A … those fucking spics!

180

And these jazz musicians … where do they get off? Sunglasses at night? Really?

You got to hand it to him. His granddaughter ran off to smoke blunts and take machine-gun-selfies with the Black Panthers and he kept the ransom money for himself! … the original Lebowski!

Fuck the rope and sail makers … we're lucky Christopher Columbus preceded him.

Fuck sustainable paper, fuel, clothes, oil and food.

Extraordinary how one man's greed could fuck things up.

Sarah Winchester knows. Hide-and-seek with apparitions for 40 years in her maze mansion.

But where there's a will for weed there's a way.

He corners me at convention. He's hunted me down. He's a big fan. Has something he has to share with me … exclusively. He's not telling anyone else … that will be my mission.

He's outdone the Swedes with their click flooring.

His idea: Just drop it and walk away … Gravity! A little Sir Isaac Newton.

Nails. Glue. Staples. Tape … for morons!

Locking systems? Why bother!

It's his concept. His patent … simply one of many! … he's making sure I acknowledge it. That I'm taking proper notes.

Rings!

Not suction cups!

… the distinction must be clear. An <u>anti-skid backer</u>!

Physics!

A smarter approach!

He would know ... PHDs from Penn State ... The Clapper ... the whole thing with "Clap on. Clap off." ... his thesis! The result of a late-night run to Radio Shack.

The circuitry in the first Xerox machine? Motion detectors? ... I was looking at *the* inventor! Here he is in the flesh.

This modest marvel ran Armstrong's research and development; he engineered their European and Asian plants ... tinkering was his thing. A wrench here; an electronic spectrometer there.

Now he's rebelling. He's throwing a capitalist tantrum ... he's over corporate flooring.

"Neurons and dendrites. Not bricks and mortar."

... his mantra.

David Reichwein. A gray suit wrapped around sunglasses twisted in a murky mind and soul.

Now he's handing me a check for $90,000.

He wants to be our best advertiser. No. More than that ... partners! He wants to partner with us ... a long-term showering of cash. This $90,000 ... just a token.

Of course, there's no business card.

Why would there be?

He's operating in the world of ideas, not matter.

The revolutionary flooring?

... just something that needed to be done! Again, *just one* of his patents.

Then he's gone.

... but I have the check!

Bzzzz. Bzzzz. Bzzzz.

... I'm calling Sandy on his cell phone. Direct.

"Sandy?"

Yeah.

"I got a new advertiser for you."

Yeah, who's that? < ---- that's him being skeptical. He's heard it before. Someone making promises so I do a little writey writey.

"FreeFit! I'm holding a check for $90,000."

Now he loves me! He's showering me with the "great jobs" and "way to knock it out of the parks" ... most of all: he wants me to overnight the check.

Where's Charlton, our overpaid sales guy? ... the only thing he knows about floors is that he walks on them with his expensive shoes.

It's rare to retire unscathed from the Too Much Fun Club ... I certainly pushed my luck. I was skating on thin Puerto Rican ice.

No one begrudged me the occasional turista. I didn't parade them around — far from it. But I got brazen. I developed a taste for locals.

It started innocently enough outside the surf clique; chatting up waitresses at the gringo-owned café, check out girls at Walmart ... but it's no use ... everyone's related or has fucked on this island.

The deepest discretion? Sincere effort?

... doesn't matter!

Inevitable detection!!!!

And with these hot heads?

No rhyme or reason!

This one's cousin.

That one's sister.

Current and former girlfriends.

Lesbians (lesbians love me).

… not sustainable! Absolutely not!

And then out of Nowhereland

… a neck.

The neck!

A slightly freckled neck connected to a freckled American face.

Look but don't touch!

She couldn't have made that more clear.

I tried. I'm the first to admit it: always pushing my luck. Taking things a bit too far. A trait. Unbecoming … in some circles.

Ring-a-ling-a-ling!!!!!!!

Ring-a-ling-a-ling!!!!

Dave Reichwein wants to play chess online.

He wants to build a relationship to milk me for free editorial content. He knows what he's doing … kind of.

A total trouncing!

Clobbered!!!

I was as bored then as I am now.

… could be doing better things.

But I have to convey.

China!

He wants me to tour his factories … Dongguan. Guangzhou … little side excursions to Hong Kong and Shanghai.

Why not? He's sort of paying … he's run up a hell of a tab at Floor Covering Weekly. $160,000 and counting … I.O.U. The full-page ads kept coming … he's going to pay sooner or later. When he gets around to it.

His American monkey boy Keith picks me up at the airport.

Hong Kong's Hollywood-style Walk of Fame; pier side … Bruce Lee's star is upside down. It's reassuring. John Lennon was right: we're not the only ones.

It doesn't take long to figure out why Keith's stuck in China … complete loser! With a hard-knock-life trash family story … biker parents. Meth.

Takes one to know one.

Speed trains. 150 miles per hour with popcorn and pretty uniformed stewardesses.

Old ladies hocking up loogies and depositing them at your feet.

1.4 billion rude Chinese people trying to box you out … out of line. Away from doorways. Entranceways and exits … they don't discriminate. Everyone for themselves! … these are some communists!

My driver says its best to back over anyone you hit … to make sure. Otherwise you're responsible for life.

Who the fuck wants that?

Chop-Suey the motherfucker!

But pull out a dollar?

…. whoa-oh-oh! …. Better hold on for your life!

The tugging.

The pulling.

… at your sleeve.

Everything's for sale!

Name brand knock- offs. Seconds. Electronics … iPods that don't work with cockroaches in them.

How many Chinamen does it take to make a laminate floor?

… 400 antique bikes lined up outside the factory.

Dormitories.

… married couples living out their lives with a bed and sink.

A late-night knock at my fancy state-run foreigners-only hotel.

… a 16 year-old Chinese Little Bo Peep and her stocky, middle-aged handler … a special delivery. Expensive plum wine. The debauchery simmered in such class.

And how very playful she is.

She giggles.

She sits on my lap.

… and then I think about all the putrid necks that have disappeared … no, disembarked. Skedaddled from me.

I'm filled with an overwhelming desire to remain pure. It pours through me. Baptized by my Freckle-Faced American girl whose angle wings I fleeting glimpsed at Surfer's Beach.

——~~~——

A NYC cop is reaching through the passenger-side window; he's lunging toward my jewel, my Freckle-Faced treasure … he's capitalizing on us being trapped in bumper-to-bumper traffic.

"No pictures!"

He's dictating law. Making it up as he goes along … New York City's skyline is temporarily off limits! We're lucky to have gotten a glimpse!

… all of this according to him! And no *please*.

Totally unjust!

Illegal and incomprehensible to an American! But it quickly sets in: there are no more Americans … Extinct! Just like the Dodo … all that remains are docile domesticated victims. Submissive and compliant to the max! Fearful! Fearful of everything foreign and domestic. Fearful of each other.

I suppress my rage while he rips the phone from her innocent, gentle hands … he's deleting images of the incomplete One World Trade Center; the scaffolding twisting its way higher into the sky.

It's an affront to my personal space. To photography's creative process. Of art. And to my intelligence.

No pictures?

Let's put aside Google Earth and the 360-degree view I can obtain, print, scan and email from the comfort of my home. But how about a NORAD response to 9/11? How about not training Mohamed Atta at Maxwell Air Force Base's International Officers School?

I know how to keep tabs on these motherfuckers. I follow up.

But this overseer (officer) of man is too simpleminded to understand cell phone photos are not the danger. Or he probably does but doesn't care … he thinks he joined the winning team and that they're not going to rob his pension; that they're going to keep him around … someone has to unclog the toilet.

Obviously, he's ignorant of robotics.

Only a matter of time … the day of the knucklehead is nearly over.

This all would've been a tremendous downer if we weren't back in the states to ask Freckly-Face's father's permission to marry.

There goes Queens and its depressing traffic jams.

There goes the Meadowbrook Parkway … Mineola, Garden City and further off Long Beach.

There goes Nassau County.

Now we're really moving. No traffic … nothing but Pine Barrens, streams and native Brook Trout. The Northern State is the way to go … they built the overpasses low, in stone, to keep the buses out. Which is to say, to keep the blacks out … their stone construction remains intact but their purpose rendered obsolete. Inundated from every angle by every race and creed … schoolgirls hooked on heroin. Muslim terrorist taxi drivers.

But this is what you call a house!

… on the other side of the forested, wrap-around driveway.

Six bedrooms! Six bathrooms! … a toilet for every ass. And St. George's Golf Course right across the street.

Mr. Freckleface isn't feeling St. George's, though … too easy! … he's all about the Nissequogue Golf Club. And washing his convertible Mercedes-Benz.

There are no "country" clubs around here … that's to keep the wives away. Just the occasional banquet.

The maître d' surfer knows Freckley-Face's twin sister. They go to the same yoga studio … everyone's a yogi now. Three- to four hours a week followed by binge alcohol consumption; $80 bottles of wine.

Even with my tie and blazer he knows I'm an imposter … "one of these things don't belong" … definitely not a member! … Just look at my left wrist … Tan! … a little too tan! … not like little Johnny over there who came to knock a few golf balls with his pops … ostentatious little fucker. His watch is three times larger than his father's … the cost? Who would know with these people… $10,000 or $120,000 … it's all the same. The decimal point doesn't matter much.

This maître d' can definitely smell my unspecialized undergrad degree. He can smell my pedigree.

I'm on to him too, though. With the surfing.

… four-foot Jobos would eat him alive!

I've never run except for Jobos. Jobos will make you run. Jobos humbles everyone sooner or later.

What happens in Hannover never happened … doesn't exist. It's not like Las Vegas … nothing stays behind; the sin is simmered to perfection. Privately.

At the Best Western King's Park Hotel … right across from the Messe Convention Center … the one with the spinning devil head atop its office tower. You wouldn't believe what was being offered over the Internet … Blondes! Every type imaginable!

Young skinny ones with small tits.

Young skinny ones with bigger and bigger tits.

… differentiated by body type and perversions.

This one will take piss and cum to the face but absolutely no ass fucking … don't ask twice. It's rude.

That one will take it in the ass for a 100 euro bonus, a little tip … but you're gonna have to cum on her tits. Or her ass. Or in the bag … the face is absolutely off limits.

Kim … a 23-year-old brunette with the most perfect body you've ever seen … curvy but tight. An athletic thin frame with an apple ass and firm C cups … she took it in the ass and the face! She had a high center of gravity … great posture … you could see her rib cage in every photo regardless of the pose.

Of course, it's her night off!

Sunday!

… she must be observant!

Cindy was a close second. A "24-year-old" blonde with the same body but her countenance — gazing off indifferently, bored — conveyed an ambivalent maturity. I absolutely suspected false advertising! Too beautiful! At 175 euro an hour she would be the world's most devalued, unrecognized commodity … like me as a writer.

Beep. Boop. Beep … ring, ring, ring … she'll be right over … that's when the panic sets in. It's real. With all the consequences … getting to feel like a letch, a whoremonger.

A rationalizer: everyone's entitled to a bachelor party now and again, no?

I was 17 when I went to my first bachelor party. I was racing pitchers of beer with my mom's cousin, a former Notre Dame offensive line captain who was huge, married and prepping for something I was totally unaware of.

In comes the groom to be with his rowdy friends!

I thought this signaled that food was on the way. That Baked Ziti and garlic bread would miraculously appear to balance out the kegs and wine coolers … It certainly wasn't my responsibility, but I needed something other than booze in my belly.

We circle up the chairs. It's like a childhood birthday party … musical chairs? Pin-the-tail-on-the-donkey? Duck … Duck … Goose?

In comes a large man cloaked in a leather trench coat and a woman. To me, at that time, she was ancient … probably 33.

She has some unique talents. She's naked on a metal folding chair blowing smoke rings with her vulva.

Now she's inserting eggs into her vagina … different colors … name a color combination in … a different combination out. Perfect accuracy! Really no different than handing you change for a $10.

America!

The Universe!

A million ways to get corrupted. On purpose!

I take the bed sheets and pillows, the padding … I toss them beside the bed. For some reason I'm overly concerned about sleeping on my spiritual mess.

I go check her picture one more time on the agency's website. I load up a clip of a similar-looking porn actress … I'm trying to transform nervous energy into sexual ecstasy.

I'm not nervous because I'm shy. I'm well past that point … it's that I know it's wrong, but I want to do it anyway. That I want to do sick things to strange women.

I lock my laptop, wallet and passport in the room's closet safe.

Everything's safe but the 250 euro I have in my pants. There's another 50 stashed in each coat pocket. It's contingency money.

I strategically set up two piles of condoms: Six besides the window, next to the mini bar … I want to keep the window curtains open, so I can look out onto the city lights, but know it will be an unnecessary discussion, a debate while I'm paying for the hour, so I close them … I put six down next to the TV, by the desk.

The agency said she would take only thirty minutes to arrive; like Domino's. I didn't believe them, but still … I was gazing out the window. I didn't want to be disappointed when I opened the door.

I see her.

I'm almost certain it's her.

I told them specifically: "Yes! The Best Western!" … "But not the main building!!!" … "The Kronsberg Residence!!!!" … "It's to the left! A separate building!"

I see her enter the rotating glass doors of the main lobby … Not bad! Nice legs! Even from way up here in my perch … she's gonna realize my room number does not correlate to that building's third floor.

I hurry down the stairs.

I cut across the parking lot.

It's snowing. It's accumulating.

There she is!

Boy is she fast! She's leaning into her pimp's passenger-side window … probably discussing how my room isn't in that building.

I didn't feel bad about it … I warned them. I made it clear.

"Cindy?"

She faces me. Fakes a smile. We walk towards the Kronsberg in the snow … It's not far … 25- to 30 yards.

We take the elevator up.

Not a word until we get into my room.

"You're not Cindy."

She insists I'm mistaken. She astonished by the accusation … Cindy or no Cindy, who would delay the absolute unfettered access?

I go to the safe. I take out my laptop. It's already opened to Cindy's page.

"That's not you!"

Now she confesses. Cindy went back to Poland.

I want to see her body. It's only fair given the bait-and-switch stunt.

She pulls up her shirt and there's nothing but flat stomach, small waist and firm titties. They're big titties, but they're young and firm … better than Cindy's.

She flashes me a smile. She has braces.

"Yea. But Cindy likes it in the ass and cum on her face" … that's me stalling. Trying to back out.

She makes it clear: I could cum on her face but absolutely no ass play.

I should take what's being *legally* offered, here. It's a good deal … It's a great deal! Instead I make a stink. The whole thing about false advertising, the loss leader.

Something inside of me can't go through with it. It's the pain-in-the-ass enlightenment … being knowledgeable … about sex slavery; about international child slavery; mind control.

Imposter Cindy is the consummate professional. She doesn't bat an eye. She doesn't flinch … a calm call from her cell phone. A little German, possibly some Polish, and right out the door.

Almost immediately my room's phone rings. It's the lady from the agency. She's handling it pretty well … once I make her admit to the Cindy switcheroo.

She's trying to renegotiate. Another blonde who likes anal is already on the way.

I tell her thanks but no thanks. The moment has passed.

Outside the window, across the freeway, I can see the devil atop the convention center still spinning; even in the dead-of-night snow.

I can go on and on but my Maybe So Agent says it's already too raunchy. That I should write more about my mother … if that ain't living in the past — on the other side of death and corruption — I don't know what is.

Nobody wants to hear about gumdrops and jellybeans … the raunchier the better! That's the motto of the day.

I'm in the right business at the wrong time. Nobody reads anymore. They're all out fucking. Or planning a big fuck.

I head over to the convention. It stopped snowing. Clear blue skies but cold … there's the devil head. I wasn't dreaming. It's still spinning … the highest point within eyesight in all directions.

The bastards won't let me in for free. I have to buy a ticket and get refunded at the press room, which is located in the heart of the spinning devil-head mausoleum.

"What's this logo?" … that's me being inquisitive upon receiving my press credentials.

"Hermes?" … that's me double checking. Making sure I got it right.

Whoever they call it, the logo's unquestionably a horned head. These Europeans were definitely over Christianity. And why not? Who wants to feel fucking guilty all the time?

You think you've seen one floor you've seen them all? … you've got to fly out to Hannover for the annual Domotex convention.

Twenty-three airplane hangars full of carpet, rugs, ceramic tile, hardwood, laminate and vinyl flooring … floors that float and click together … glue down floors … softer floors, harder floors, cheaper floors and the most expensive lavish floors you could dream of. Elaborate rugs … 20-foot polished wood planks. Europeans. Americans. Asians. Arabs … there's not too many blacks in the flooring business.

Pig knuckle is the other major attraction in Hannover. That, and the bordellos … they don't call them bordellos. They're clubs … Yes Sir, Haus 66, Harem XI and Reitwallsex. There's also the Marktkirche… the church with the inverted pentagram steeple.

The thing to do is to go downtown, by the train station, have pig knuckle and several tall glasses of beer … stroll towards the church … very nonchalant … to see the sights … you only inadvertently wind up in Yes Sir. It's understandable, being right there on the corner. A large stone façade. All very high end.

Up a flight of stairs … I'm greeted by an old witch who escorts me to the red-lit lounge. Very comfy couch!

Drink?

"No thanks."

How polite!

One at a time the girls enter in their bra and panties … they shake my hand. They introduce themselves and then file into ranks, like soldiers for inspection.

This one's too chubby.

That one's too chubby and too old.

That blonde is hot but looks a little used up. The brunette got a little skinny ass.

I go with the blonde in her 20s.

We're in a private room. Red and black décor with lace and candles … there's a bed and two chairs … we agree on a couple hundred euro for an hour, all inclusive.

She disappears with my money to get change.

I start thinking … Here I go again. My biggest crime: noodling things over in my mind.

I step out of the room. I'm embarking on a little hide and seek.

This is highly irregular. No one needs to tell me … I'm interfering. I could compromise another client's confidentiality.

It doesn't take long for granny to intercept me. Just a few steps … she politely drags me back to the lounge; she's talking in hushed tones; essentially inquiring what the fuck is wrong with me. Why can't my amateur American ass get with the program?

I tell her I changed my wind. I want the skinny one. The one with the bony ass.

She smiles at me. I amused her. Now she understands … everyone is entitled to change their mind.

She calls for Natascha who nearly instantly materializes. There she is … Tall. Tight. Pretty.

I change my mind again. Now I want my money back.

They're more than happy to oblige. She can't stuff it in my hand fast enough … anything to keep me from dancing back and forth in the hallway. Anything to get me out; immediately!

The night became still. The snow had stopped but Hermes was still spinning when I got back to the hotel. Despite my efforts I was still pure. Or at least no more tainted than when I first arrived.

CHAPTER 19:

⸻ ❧ ⸻

CAN I SELL YOU?

"For our struggle is not against flesh and blood, but against the rulers, against the authorities, against the powers of this dark world and against the spiritual forces of evil in the heavenly realms." — Ephesians 6:12

Everything was perfect. I pretty much had everything … then she convinced me we needed more. And then the phone rang.

Dave Reichwein … now he wants to fly me to Lancaster. He's pushing his luck. There's a reason I moved to Puerto Rico … *Los siento … Yo necesito voy … Hasta Luego.*

He won't accept *no*. The flights already booked! A car waiting on both ends.

… a long sunflower-lined driveway.

… a fully functional farm, really: horses, cows, turkey and corn.

The most important thing now is shooting the Barrett .50 caliber tank killer.

I must!

All business is postponed until I fire.

… right there off the ranch's back deck. Prone. Between the wood railings.

The bullet is six inches long but they swear I won't feel the kick … "just slightly" … "Mediocre" … "The best place to be is behind it" … that's Rich, the retired special-forces operator and Black Water employee. Multi-tours to the Middle East … his job: construct a first-class outdoor gun range on the property … beautifully con-structed log-and-earth backstops at multiple ranges. Metal gongs of all sizes. Spinning metal plates and clay-pigeon tossers … targets fly-ing here, there and everywhere.

Donald, Reichwein's "partner" in bringing in containers of ammo and tanks from Poland, handed me an automatic M4. He's the son of a colonel with an irregularly large bulbous head. The army rejected him because he had flat feet.

"We sell the tanks to collectors," said Reichwein. "We pour con-crete down their barrels except for the ones we sell to China for target practice."

But now that I fired the Barrett it's time to get down to brass tactics. He's making me an offer … $120,000 a year … an Audi RS5 … it's right over there (black with tan leather interior) … he wants me to represent FreeFit in the New York City area … besides him, who better to do it? Who else knows the product, the company and its customers so well?

"Just be yourself," he said.

I could handle that. I've seen some of these over-paid knuckle-head salespeople. Real buffoons!

… still.

…. a little suspicious how his last sales guy just disappeared; won-dered off.

"Problems at home. His wife won't let him travel."

I believe it! I caught him red handed in Las Vegas and Shanghai ... chance encounters at hotel elevators and bars.

There really wasn't much to discuss. We both knew he was doing me a favor ... Freckly Face back home was getting a little over the island life anyway ... especially with the locals poisoning our dog Trotter; and the barefoot kids giving us death stares as we traverse the dirt road to Surfers Beach. Our presence was the offense ... outside of the surf community, which generally viewed us as friendly, fun, generous: 100% colonists! ... you name it, it was our fault! ... doesn't matter their society was built on American cars, cell phones, power lines, computers ... it didn't dawn on them that they were speaking Spanish an awfully long way from Madrid ... not a Taino in site ... Gringos Go Home!

I would need a week or two to figure out the relocation ... it's not just me anymore with my three surfboards, a few books, antique typewriter and laptop. Now I got a wife ... three dogs. Wedding plate sets and cookery ... fancy stuff ... did you see her dad's house? ... I'll be needing that $120,000 a year real soon!

Dave Reichwein doesn't want to hear it. From now on all he wants are results.

He gives me $10,000 for the move and another $10,000 for clothes; a plane ticket home; and the keys to the new black Audi with tan leather interior.

—∞—

Back in The States it's like an archaeological dig. Americans trying to excavate a racism that was buried in the '60s; all but extinct except for the hardest, wickedest hearts by the '70s.

And there's a new fascination with bathrooms ... with letting men use the women's room.

Your child's XY chromosomed gym instructor ... 100% allowed to shower with your 12-year-old daughter!

Don't ask about it!

No inquiries!

The slightest reproach:

"Racist!"

"Homophobe!"

They dare you to say it. They want you to rebuke them … on camera! … everyone's a Bodhisattva George Lukas … they want to get you fired from your job!

XY married to XY … perfect contenders to adopt! As many young boys as they can feed.

Moms dressing their sons like JonBenét Ramsey; taking them to the public library for a nap lullaby by the local transsexual clown.

Nothing is more virtuous.

Boy these are good people.

They love you enough to let you kill your baby in the ninth month. Hell … they'll encourage you to wait! … they'll put it on ice for you … organs to the highest bidder … AMZN has nothing on post-birth organ tissue.

Mary Gatter's holding out for a Lamborghini.

She's the De Beers of aborted babies.

Hope and Change.

Anwar Al-Awlaki was hoping for his right to Due Process.

It wasn't played up in the media … not with the Associated Press having their phones tapped.

Everyone's little sins recorded forever. Or own premature Day of Judgement … they're not waiting for you to slip up … they already got the fall on tape … audio and visual!

Selling machine guns to Mexican Cartels … Spying on the Tea Party. Siccing the IRS on his political rivals … good thing Obama is black!

The ruling class!

You can keep your doctor … Benghazi … hidden computer servers.

Little fibs. White lies.

A few Hail Mary's at most.

No one even notices. They're dumping buckets of ice water on their heads.

I told you. A new America … super virtuous! You've never seen people so good … with their ass out at Walmart. Stealing packages off your porch … I told you. Everything recorded 24/7.

Definitely anti-Nazi!

They've made that clear.

… and anti-fascist!

It's hard to tell so they're beating the hell out of everyone. Even each other … these Soros' numbskull organizers sometimes double book.

Definitely Hope for some … the future looks bright for perverts and debauchers. Blood thirsty baby killers … celebrants of evil, really.

Change for all.

… that's obvious.

Whether you like it or not.

With all this money and a new fancy car, it was time to do something dramatic … 1,300 miles to Kansas City.

Again with the dreary Queens traffic, the Bronx … massive potholes, many dented fenders and side panels; golf balls on wheels, really … Graffitied trucks and deliver vans. Graffitied walls, overpasses, store fronts and apartment buildings … Graffitied everything … un-healed casualties of the urban environment.

The Bronx.

The George Washington Bridge.

West through Jersey and Pennsylvania's farmland … granite tun-nels burrowed through the Allegheny Mountains.

Cincinnati. Louisville. St Louis. Columbia. Kansas City … the cit-ies line up on the GPS. Pushing further and further into the night … Delirious coffee tremors balanced with weed and podcast radio.

Careful not to mistakenly pump gasoline!

After 15- or 16 hours at the wheel it's easy to forget: diesel only with this prima donna automobile.

… shaky hands and heavy eyelids at 3:00 a.m.

… 18-wheelers fanned out in parking lots sleeping; degenerates raiding the 24-hour shelves.

All that way and Big Bob could care less about the Newtonian-inspired physics of FreeFit … more than happy to see me, but as far as he's concerned, we could go fuck ourselves with this no-skid backer.

Who needs it?

He's buying up everyone's overstocked inventory for pennies on the dollar. He's handing me thin-rolled joints of old Mexican weed … his trophy wife laying a couple scoops of vanilla ice cream on our soon-to-be-served apple pie.

Now this is work I can do!

I found the right field!

But now it's 1,300 miles back and the phone won't stop ringing.

Mike Roetelle, FreeFit's technical director — which is to say he's an old installer who's knees and back gave out after 40 years so now he "consults," "advises," anything other than get back on his knees

— he wants to know if I've been paid. So does Mathew Fooshee, FreFit's Mid-West representative based in Houston; and James Contreras, our West Coast counterpart … apparently everyone's more than a month behind in salary and expense reimbursements.

Uh oh.

But before I could call Reichwein to get a grasp of the situation he calls me with a couple questions of his own, namely, how many containers of FreeFit is Big Bob going to buy?

I spread the truth. I know the person I really need to sell is the one signing my check.

"He wants me to show it to his two largest partners: Vinnie Virga up in Connecticut and Scott Apple in Lancaster. He wants to know what they think."

Reichwein wants me to know what *he* thinks. He's made it perfectly clear: Where's the fucking PO (purchase order)?

"The key to getting rich," he says, "is making your employer and his associates boatloads of money. Handing over bags of cash."

I get it. Trickle-down economics with me at the bottom. Surprise. Surprise.

The best bet for me closing a sale, he said, would be driving a complete set of our latest introductions up to Jeff Knowles in Toronto. He's already expressed interest in the longer, wider planks.

A qualified lead! A distributor who's good for 10- to 12 containers a year; though Reichwein insists that they're doing 20 and should be doing 40.

I pack the car; I roll enough joints to get me to the Canadian border.

The whole thing with the Queens, Bronx, George Washington Bridge … blah, blah, blah, blah, blah, blah, blah. But now I'm heading north! NY 17 and NY 90 past the Catskills. Fall colors.

I'm barely out of Westchester when you know who's already asking about the PO … where is it? When is he going to get it?

I'm reminding him of the plan. The samples in my car. East Setauket to Toronto … only two hours into an 11-hour drive.

A bit of unexpected congestion on the Thru Way. Everyone's tapping their breaks … and then I tap my breaks to sneak a better glimpse of the armored black Homeland Security bus; several similarly adorned armored vehicles; and a group of black-glad commandos parked on a wide, grassy shoulder.

They're fixing for something. A practice run.

More than one genius is going to try to evacuate the city when the jig is finally up.

When it is, they'll be waiting for you right there.

Either to boot you back into play or scoop you up to Never Never Land. Bon-Voyage.

It didn't take long … less than two months.

James Contreras on the West Coast … Gone! Kaput! … he couldn't cut it.

"He's out there sucking his thumb," said Reichwein. "He's sitting in his underwear waiting for the phone to ring. He's jerking off in front of the computer."

That's one way of seeing it.

Another could be that the gravity floor was failing. It would shrink when it got cold. It would expand when it got hot … consistent temperature or live with unsightly gaps or trip-inducing peaked ends. It's your choice … 65° to 85° … that was your 20° window. Deal with it.

Because it said so in the manual — which no self-respecting installer ever read — Mr. Reichwein told B.R. Funsten, the largest West

Coast distributor, to go fuck itself when it came to claims. He didn't want to hear it … as far as he's concerned: FreeFit's the perfect floor! His invention!

He'll admit, the first generation of double-sided tape — to secure the perimeter; hold the puzzle together … a bit of an oopsido … actually melted the vinyl backing, slicked it up like Vaseline … certainly didn't help hold these moving floors in place.

That's fixed now! He's adamant about it! As long as the installers use the right glue or tape. And the right size trowel … Not too wide. Not too narrow … definitely the Goldilocks of flooring.

James Contreras didn't stand a chance.

B.R. Funsten tossed the displays and bad mouthed us to everyone! To anyone who would listen!

Mike Roetelle was next … We didn't need a technical director to explain why we wouldn't settle claims. We just didn't … "Sorry. You used the wrong adhesive."

The real pickle was when they used the right adhesive and it still failed … no rhyme or reason. Curling on the ends. Either arching it's back like a swan dive or doing an impression of Downward Dog … I've even seen it try to curl itself lengthwise into a noodle.

It was my job to find something.

… a crack in the subfloor.

… too much space around the perimeter.

… not enough space around the perimeter.

Most important? … check the temperature!

Discreetly spy the thermostat setting … mostly likely it's not even installed yet in a commercial setting … lick your finger and stick it up in the air … I shoot my temperature laser down where the wall meets the floor by the window. I can see the snow outside … 47° subfloor!

"Are you trying to freeze us?"

Or at your house … "Of course there are gaps!" … "Of course there's lifting!" … "Obviously the installers didn't acclimate the floor for 48 hours."

They admit it … the installers just showed up and got right to it … in and out … there was no acclimating as far as they're concerned … at least definitely not here … maybe somewhere else.

"But that doesn't do us any good." … I explain the extreme warehouse temperatures. The back of trucks in February and July.

Did they stack the cartons flat on top of each other or lean them against the wall?

It matters!

Vinyl memory!

It's very simple … it's everybody else's fault.

What part of "Claim Denied" do you not understand?

… no doubt our little gravity floor was costing distributors hundreds of thousands of dollars and a whole lot of Good Will in the marketplace.

… retailers … contractors … refusing to buy so much as a screw from them until their FreeFit claims were settled … the spigot was turned completely off … no drip drip.

Mathew Fooshee simply couldn't take it any more … his accountant wife nagging about the delinquent paychecks; Reichwein calling all hours of the day and night.

It was horrible. But I learned I could deal with horrible for $120,000 a year under the table. $10,000 a month tax free.

I flew out to Seattle and opened up Cascade Pacific … two locations … Seattle and Portland … two containers a piece … $200,000.

I was able to convince Tony Benvenuti at WoodPro that it was worth bringing in six containers and dividing them between his New England and Floridian warehouses … "these other distributors just weren't doing it right. Wrong glue! … always the problem."

Tony's two top guys had a great time at Reichwein's farm ... they broke out the M19 Browning belt-fed machine gun ... as the finale ... after silenced shot guns, MP4s and the Barrett .50 caliber ... any opportunity to use it. $3.50 a round ... Marine Recon Rich doesn't let those opportunities go to waste ... he rigs up some Amish furniture with explosives ... when one of the distributor reps finally hit the target ... K-A-B-O-O-M!!! ... a huge blast. A mushroom cloud.

... but look!

... the FreeFit.

... not too badly damaged! Even after that.

Reichwein's peeling out over FreeFit with his Porsche 918 ... it's staying put ... visible wear? Sure. A melted hole right through the center. But the remaining surface layer looked good.

I'd be impressed if I wasn't taking 10 claim calls a day.

Ohio Valley and Adleta were still buying from us ... two of the powerhouse distributors that didn't drop us ... four- to five containers a month between the two of them ... it would be more if they didn't hate us.

They were caught in Reichwein's Chinese Finger Trap ... they invested heavily upfront and brought in 10 containers each plus hundreds of displays. They pushed it onto their customers and now it was failing 40 percent of the time ... we told you, when it comes to claims: No Habla Ingles ... yet there remained *some* demand. It takes some time for bad news to set in. No one wants to face reality ... the distributors spent a year praising FreeFit. The dealers wanted to believe it could be so simple ... no more bonehead installers ... no one wanted to admit they'd been duped. Especially me.

Now Reichwein's buying horses, more Porsches and an executive touring bus ... he rolls into meetings like Led Zeppelin ... it only pisses everyone off. All their claims being denied and he's showing off his new $20,000 Special Forces-trained German Shepard.

Ohio Valley and Adleta start cutting back on their monthly container purchases … now they're buying overstock FreeFit for pennies on the dollar from the other distributors that can't stand to look at it in their warehouses. It disgusted them.

The writing was on the wall.

The GREENGUARD Environmental Institute is calling. They want to know why we're still using their logo … and that we owe them $50,000.

"We're phthalate free!"

"We're GREENGUARD Certified."

"We only use healthy, natural plasticizers" … "no shrunken balls or cancer."

That was my spiel.

Reichwein would take it a step further.

"Virgin vinyl," he said.

"We'll buy it back," he said.

That was a good one until Ohio Valley asked to sell back $150,000 of carpet-tile visuals that had collected dust.

The money fucks with your head. All kinds of screwy things start making sense.

A $550 leather Orvis brief case ... to match the stack of new pants, wrinkle-free shirts and ridiculously expensive shooting jacket … a true sport coat. With twin big pockets at the waist; to hold boxes of ammo. Patches on the elbows. Special slits tailored into the shoulder blades to comfortably swing a shotgun … it truly is magnificent.

New Orvis waders and wading boots ... Vest. Rod and reel. The fancy wood-handled rubberized net. It's less stressful for the fish you've dragged to your feet … Flies … lots of flies.

$2,000 Benelli Ethos.

… I barely know how to load it. There's buttons and levers. Reversable safety, barrel breech and multiple fiber-optic colored sights. I got the engraved nickel-plated version with the patented Inertia-Driven recoil reduction system. The manual's in Italian.

A real gentlemanly act I got going. I even got two watches. A black and gold wide-faced, waterproof Rip Curl; and a small, antiqued, gold-faced, leather-banded Orvis.

I'm amongst two-bit salesmen standing at the corner of our respective convention center booths, looking positive. Never the slightest hint that our numbers are off … our numbers are always off. Management wants miracles. A new Olympic record every quarter.

And when the convention hall clears out, a moment of respite … take a seat! Definitely want to sit down after standing in dress shoes for 10 hours … but only for a minute. A quick breath of air … gallop back to your room. Wipe your swamp ass. A fresh shower or at least water on your face … don't sit on the bed! It's super tempting … you'll never get up … now you have to be the life of the party … all smiles for customers as you pay for their steaks, lobsters, bottles of wine, shots, desserts, coffees … this is just the warmup. The pregame show … then off to shows, nightclubs, strip clubs … all of the above! … these sons-of-bitches don't have to be standing in the booth tomorrow morning at 8:00 a.m.

Escorts in and out of the lobby. Up and down elevators … it's the only time these guys get laid. Their wives? Stone statues also taking advantage of the expense account … if it was up to them their husbands would never come home.

Countless exhausted highway miles.

Broken white lines feeding into the center of your consciousness.

Blinding lights in the review.

Blinding lights from oncoming traffic.

Coffee tremors.

Rest Stop sink showers to throw water on your face … water down the wrists and back of your neck.

Cops behind you with flashing lights.

Cops requesting you step out of the car. Inquisitive motherfuckers … mainly they want to know about the air freshener dangling from the rear-view mirror; it concerns them … these interstate highways? Might as well be named Pablo Escobar Thruway.

What am I trying to hide?

Why didn't I roll the window all the way down?

This guy's no fool.

… he can smell something skunky.

I tell him I'm scared of the police.

… Have good reason to be.

… Has he seen the riots; the police beatings in Ferguson?

It's the best sale I made all week.

Then I get home unaware that my wife was pregnant and I would soon lose my six-figure job.

CHAPTER 20:

MOTHERFUCKER OF THE YEAR

"Hard work spotlights the character of people: some turn up their sleeves, some turn up their noses, and some don't turn up at all." — *Sam Ewin*

The move and career change were predicated on having a baby so I was finally getting laid … and it was great sex! … procreation sex! … absolutely the best!

We see the doctors. We share our plan … natural childbirth all the way! … Breast feeding, it goes without saying … Freckley Face is insulted that it needs to be said … what else should be expected of a hippie surfer girl?

Of course, the doctors push back on the vaccines. They insist he needs to be a pin cushion from the get go. For his safety. The safety of the community. For school … it's mandatory they said.

I do a little pushing myself. I came prepared. I was expecting it … I hold the law, religious exemption under their nose. When I do something, I do it all the way. I have the vaccine inserts … complete with the listed side effects … autism isn't skyrocketing for nothing … 1 out of 54 kids born with blank stares; one-day adults in diapers.

Armed with data … the doctors don't like that … mercury levels vs FDA recommendations … for adults, never mind newborns. Aluminum. Formaldehyde … it boils down to *because they tell you so.*

It doesn't help that my wife's mother is a retired nurse … these nurses … you'd think they're doctors … 100% institutionalized! … unwitting pharmaceutical sell outs, the lot of them.

I've had multiple surfer doctor friends over the years, including Freckley Face's twin sister's most recent gold-digging expedition, a brain expert: "Whatever you do, don't vaccinate your kid."

You think Bill Gates and Steve Jobs vaccinate their kids? You think they let them near their billion-dollar gadgets …. What are you? Vaccinated?

⁓

The entire plan is out the window … it didn't take long. Back in the states around her Long Island sisters for three months … Starbucks. New York House Wives. The Kardashians … now the natural childbirth has been scheduled. Like a moon landing. We have a date and time.

Forget the "push. push. push" in the films … 100% zonked out of her mind with an epidural. It's over before she knew it began … she's so far gone she can't hold our newborn son … for two days … forget breastfeeding … I'm fighting with the nurses to hydrate my raisin. He's parched. His mother's out cold. They couldn't pump milk if they wanted to.

There I am … 72 hours standing in as a crib in the corner chair. They finally bring me a bottle … me and my little potato.

The other moms … our nation's little guests from Guatemala, Honduras, El Salvador, China … from everywhere but here …

our entire floor: It's a Small World After All … and on our dime … they're up and at 'em … 48 hours and they're walking around. They're doing laps around the maternity ward. But not our princes. She's still out.

When she finally comes to … her sisters fill her in … my male toxicity with the nurses … her mother was right about me … I am a loose cannon … watch your fucking toes.

When we finally get home … guess who's shift it is? … permanently mine!

Less than a year at the new job and as parents; we wore out our welcome at the golf-course mansion … and it wasn't just me.

Freckley Face's mother was getting on everyone's nerves … Munchhausen's … I don't know what it is with me and significant other's moms and the phony baloney diseases. First Amie's with the Fibromyalgia … the everywhere pain from nowhere … and now this lunatic.

Every possible elective surgery!

A former nurse, she knew how to tamper with the tests; she knew exactly what to say … diagnosis? … 100% horrible 100% of the time.

She already gave up half a kidney. The whole family on pins and needles when something actually goes wrong someday … who's coughing up their half?

It didn't help that she was 160 lbs overweight … sedentary? … that's too many syllables to attribute to her lifestyle.

Everyone agreed … a psychological disorder related to the tragic death of her young son.

100% in need of constant sympathy … pity … she can't meet someone without working her loss into the conversation … as soon as possible! ... they need to know! The sooner, the better ... The butcher. The mailman. The pizza parlor ... especially the pizza parlor ... the owner just lost a brother in a car wreck ... common ground! Sorrow! ... but hers is the unbeatable topper! Got to give it to her!

Her other card: Al-Anon ... she'll toss it on the table right after she tells you about her son ... a triple sufferer! ... Her father: Irish alcoholic cop! ... Her husband, Freckley Face's father ... two loves: Golf and getting shit faced ... both out of the way before noon.

Daily meetings.

Big announcements when she's leaving ... We know! ... It's the only time she leaves the house. That and for the doctors.

In less than a year we've dealt with a fake broken wrist ... she won't share the X-rays. She just wears the brace ... Lyme Disease ... the neighbor's kid got it ... a week later, so does she ... it's her other specialty ... she can't let anyone suffer alone. She'll catch your cold over the phone.

It's amazing. After a week of no one giving a shit ... the Lyme Disease clears up. It disappears. Not a mention ... Edgar Cayce would be impressed. Now she has it; now she don't.

A blown ACL ... this was cutting in on my dance ... my evening icings after jui-jitsu ... fuck that! She'd show me ... wrapped like a mummy ... ankle to hip. Crutches to get from the bed to the kitchen table ... hobbling to and from Al-Anon.

Freckley Face was busy ... definitely not playing with my son ... 100% her mom's au pair.

And never enough!

Chauffeuring to and from meetings, surgeries ... the grocery store for staples; the butcher for select meats; the wine store ... Al-Anon or not; she definitely joined the nightly party at the mansion ... bottoms up all the way around at that house.

It dawned on me. There may be more to the Munchhausen's than sympathy ... the pills ... she's into them. On a drop of a dime she can turn from singing with the iPad to accusing Freckley Face and I of freeloading.

Her father is not a fool and quite reasonable; a practical man.

He confides in us: "Your mother is not well."

We know what he means.

Time to go … again. Another move. This one not transatlantic. A little hop. A skip really.

I push for Long Beach.

Familiar ground.

Much closer to the city.

A simple train ride in the a.m. Half the distance … and a little too far for her mother to pop in unannounced.

Perfect!

We go look at a couple apartments. Something within our new budget.

Even with the $120K … pickings are slim. A two bedroom here or there with crowded on street parking. Only $3,500 a month … lucky us!

Freckley Face won't have it.

Definitely "too urban."

I get back from my through-the-grinder commute … her and her father found the solution … three-bedroom, two-bath cottage with fireplace sitting on 2 acres in Connecticut. With a classic detached red barn with overhead office … *and* wood burning stove.

How am I going to pay for all of this?

Of course. Us men. We keep it to ourselves.

The house.

The two cars.

The insurance on the two cars.

… you know they take money out of the check for medical and dental, right?

The phones. The internet … The wine!!!

Out from under her mother's nose … the wine really started to flow. And not the cheap stuff.

It's all starting to weight on me.

I'm bleeding out my ass … literally! … bloody shits!

Ulcerative Colitis … you don't want it!

Medical terms being used …"urgency" … "pressure" … "polyps".

You can say that again.

Don't fart!

You never had swamp ass like this.

All I needed now was an ambush call from Kevin Jablon … I knew it wasn't going to be good. He never calls.

The founder, president and CEO of my largest customer wants to know What The Fuck Happened?

… leading question if I ever heard one.

My stomach rumbles.

There's the "urgency" … the "pressure."

I'm above the barn pacing between my desk and wood-burning stove trying not to shit myself.

"I'm going to ruin you and your family!"

No dillydallying with him.

Straight to the point!

He's absolutely furious!

… Well, it won't take much of a hex. We're holding on by a thin, frayed thread.

CHAPTER 21:

AFRAID NOT

"Better to live on a corner of the roof than share a house with a quarrelsome wife." — Proverbs 25:24

I dodged another bullet … handed another golden ticket at the last second.

"Dave, I'm sorry … Marazzi made me an offer. It's too good to turn down."

Just in time too. That FreeFit house of cards was on fire … nobody had to touch a thing. No breeze needed. Its imminent collapse was self-evident. It had begun.

He offered me more money. Three years guaranteed at $145,000 a year … I should have taken it … when it comes to sales: constant pins and needles. The end is always near … that didn't hit home yet. A string of bad luck, I thought … it's easy to get blinded … Marazzi and a reliable $120,000 a year … More than enough! Why be greedy?

I'd impressed Marazzi's vice president Hector Narvaez while working for that fruit loop Reichwein … Ohio Valley Flooring, a large mutual distributor of ours, said I was the only redeeming factor, the only reason they hadn't dropped FreeFit.

It was another double-edged sales sword.

Worldwide leader in ceramic flooring! No doubt about it!

Division of Mohawk Industries!

Mohawk bought up the flooring world. You name it … carpet, wood, ceramic, vinyl, laminate … I told you! World leader!

… one little glitch. A small one.

Marazzi had switched to SAP … the premier German software responsible for integrating all facets of the business. It would give us an unprecedented advantage over the market we already dominated … our only true competitor: Warren Buffet at Shaw … our two flooring dynasties gobbling up the entire pie.

Only problem … no one knew how to use SAP… even if they did; glitches up the wazoo.

Did we say we had that in inventory? Out to you in three days? … our mistake … this fucking SAP … won't ship until 90 days … we're making more … we're scheduling production now … a little hiccup.

We redefined the word "confirmed."

Nobody believed us anymore.

Hospital wings, university halls … hard to coordinate shutting down facilities and bringing in labor when nobody knows when the flooring will arrive … if it will arrive … intact … we couldn't tell you if the trucks were coming or going.

Mohawk purchased Marazzi, moved its headquarters to Texas … but the Italian designers … they didn't want hillbillies for neighbors.

Nobody wanted to buy what we're making even if we could get it to them.

Didn't help that everyone was now shipping in their product, EVERYTHING, direct from China … who needs domestic production? … even bringing it in all the way from over there … Can't beat the price. Not even close ... don't have to tell us about the advantages of slave labor. We're standing on it.

My territory?

Get a big desk. We'll spread out the map.

The tip of Maine down to West Virginia; West to Buffalo, NY ... Portland, Burlington, Boston, Manchester, Providence, Saratoga Springs, Albany, Syracuse, Hartford, Syracuse, Rochester ... I already mentioned Buffalo, Cheektowaga ... Philadelphia, Trenton, Atlantic City, Wilmington, Morgantown, Charleston.

Certain chunks were off limits.

New York City, Long Island, Washington, D.C. ... exclusive to our company-owned stores ... Don't worry. If we haven't already, we're opening a company-owned store near you ... you can choose: Mom and pop retailers through our distributor ... or direct from us at a 30 percent discount?

My customers loved it. Loved to point it out to me ... perfect excuse not to bring in inventory. Why stock up for tomorrow? ... they'll call me when they need me ... that's the advantage of domestic production, right?

The entire distributor sales team down 40 percent when I came on board.

... they didn't mention that in the interview.

Management didn't come down on us too hard. They heard it directly from the distributors:

"Fuck you and your SAP; your company owned stores; and your ugly floors."

They did stop complaining about price, the customers ... We moved production to China, too ... when in Rome ... or more appropriately, Shanghai ... we're all dropping our pants ... and we're all still making boat loads of money. Or at least the companies.

Still, there is tremendous nervous tension … these sales managers … Olympic Records! … Every quarter! … I told you already about their expectations.

Profits are huge but they're down … and the greedy bastards that signed on for SAP, launched the company-owned-store initiatives … they're not even considering cutting their salary. Anybody but them can go.

All this pressure … I confess … room service blowjobs from Backpage … a blowjob a quarter staves off the divorce lawyer.

The things we tell ourselves!

I told my wife I wasn't ready to be a eunuch at 40 … that a sexless cohabitation was unsustainable.

She didn't care. As long as the money kept pouring in … better someone else than her … sex was the last thing on her mind … not with a new season of Vanderpump Rules being released … her and her two sisters … constant glasses of wine and text updates … about their make-believe Reality TV friends … my son only sees daylight when I get home.

I couldn't be more invested now. The next election … what a line up. Another Bush and Clinton. Royal dynasties are just what we need.

Bush's campaign: we should vote for him because, well, he's a Bush … three time's a charm … it's nice to have the CIA and Lizard People on your side.

Clinton argues she was running the country while Bill was wetting his cigars. Her record speaks for itself … the little Benghazi lie while Secretary of State … what difference does that make?

Obviously a two-horse race. The Bohemian Grove homosexual pedophiles have decided … like always … everything else is pretense.

It's not helping that Julian Assange keeps leaking Hillary and her associate's e-mails ... all of their perversions front and center ... Podesta absolutely euphoric over Marina Abramovic's upcoming se- men- and blood-drinking party! ... he wants to know how many kids will be in the hot tub ... will they be compliant?

Good thing they got Assange locked up and banned Alex Jones ... Mums the word!

Could you imagine if everyone knew they were torturing kids for their adrenochrome?

There's a communist running, too. We're told they don't exist in the Democratic Party but here he is ... well, he calls himself a so- cialist but what's semantics? ... what's a honeymoon in the Soviet Union? ... no better place to consecrate a marriage than under a Lenin statue.

His party is already flip flopping and they haven't even won yet ... they haven't learned to keep their mouths shut ... one day they assure us they have no interest in Americans' guns; the next they're insisting the Second Amendment, the entire Constitution, is outdated ... if the guns aren't turned in millions of American deer hunters will be arrested ... sling shots and bow and arrows ... progressiveness!

They're absolutely clear about one thing: they want you to pay for everything!

Their ceramic pottery degree ... their abortions ... their tattoos, blue-hair dye and rent ... they're tired of living with mommy who hogs the large-screen TV ... they really don't want to pay for any- thing. That's their position.

I try to get through to the debates ... I got a question ... Weed? Pussy? ... who's subsidizing it? ... they may have an additional voter on their hands. I'm willing to learn Chinese.

There's a crazy outlier, though ... he's throwing a monkey wrench into the pedophiles' plan.

Donald Trump!

He's taken a step or two down with the whole reality TV "You're fired" gig … his hotels and casinos must be hurting. He must have a few bills to pay … but now he's running for president.

His Phase 1 Attack Strategy: find the most irredeemable qualities of his opponents and label them with catch-phrase nicknames.

He could have simply stopped at Bush. You'd think that would've been enough … but no: Low Energy Jeb … Crooked Hillary … got to say … he's got a good eye.

I was excited … this would be my first election. Back in the states and making six figures … would never have imagined it … it was my duty. And it was clear: Anyone but Hillary Clinton.

My Maybe So Literary Agent doesn't like my newfound political leaning … just like that: "Nice knowing you."

It's not easy to get published these days without toe sox.

You better develop a taste for soymilk.

There's something about these new Democratic Liberals … the title … it doesn't fit.

When I was a young liberal we wanted to Free Tibet … now they're praising Apple and Google for helping the Chinese spy on their citizens.

Try getting around a Subaru Outback with a Hillary- or Bernie for President sticker … absolutely refuse to get over … backing up traffic for miles … they own the road and if you don't like it: Go Fuck Yourself.

It's dangerous to disagree with them. I don't own a MAGA hat. I'm not a fan … I just call balls and strikes … my liberal pedigree couldn't be purer: son of a Democratic Cuban coke dealing painter … a pothead, weed-smoking, Deadhead surfer myself.

But these liberals are no longer loving … they'll hit you with a bike lock … they think they're fighting Nazis and Fascist … it's a mass role playing game / amateur art performance they're forcing the rest of us to participate in … this is what you get when you give everyone a trophy. They don't know they're losers.

… or maybe they do.

… and that's the point.

… they want to flip the board over and rewrite the rules so they can win without trying.

My son. I cradle him in my arms … I gently stroke his face … I caress him while feeding him his bottle … I'm aware these moments won't last.

I tuck him in … I'm 100% against it … what other mammal would abandon their newborn baby and leave it lying amongst inanimate objects? Plastic shapes, flashing lights, swinging pendulums and spinning distractions … babies need their moms.

I was overruled by Freckley Face's family, friends and social media … that's what dictated what went on in the household I supported.

I bit my tongue.

I chose my battle.

… Keep their fucking vaccinating hands off my son … at least until he's three.

There was a silent truce.

They didn't push. Especially her mother … she was scared of me. She called it exactly right: Loose! … Canon!

I'd stare at my son … Peaceful. Angelic … breathing calm and naturally from his belly … then I'd run downstairs … quick … force myself to sleep because in an hour or two he'd be up again … Da-Da … Da-Da … he knows who's coming with the bottle … you know who won't even consider it … don't bother nudging her … not after staying up to see who closed the big deal on Million Dollar Listing.

But those days were over.

I was no longer needed to carry him upstairs … no need to rock him to sleep.

Now Despicable Me … I, II and III … Wall-E … Frozen … Sing … any number of substitutes while he holds his own bottle mesmerized by the screen … when he passes out … usually around 11p.m. … I carry him to my old bed … him and Freckley Face … they both make it clear: No Daddy.

I'm on the couch for months. I get a bright idea … I can sleep in the upstairs guest room, on a bed, if I bring an empty 52-ounce bottle to piss in … to avoid traversing the steep, narrow stairwell … potentially waking the boy and prima donna … this ancient Connecticut cottage … it was designed poorly … slanted 45-degree brickwork … petrified 2" x 12" supporting beams … I don't see it lasting. Gravity will win.

The one good thing … I'm off the night shift … if I'm cut out she can deal with the dirty diapers herself. She can do a little coo, coo, coo.

Of course, the resentment has reached a boiling point on both sides.

Pointing out that 10+ hours of TV is too much for anyone, especially a three-year old … that daily day drinking isn't acceptable: 100% abusive! … male toxicity! … could I be more insensitive?

I spend $5,000 on counseling … it's the only thing that can get her to stay, not move back into her parents' mansion … a single mother with no job or employment record … she never was a contemplator.

I know it's not going to work out when he asks if I considered the risk my wife took giving birth … did I? … absolutely miniscule compared to the potential bodily harm I subject myself to on America's highways … daily.

I need someone to talk sense into this woman!

Not only am I right … I'm the victim being wrongfully accused of abuse! … I'm no longer allowed an opinion … she made it clear: I'm not interested in hearing anymore of your crackpot ideas … about the New World Order … about aliens … Satanists … mind control … and most of all vaccines.

The time has come!

I was able to keep their damn hands off him for three years.

They knew I wasn't fucking around … I didn't do all that research, collect all those vaccine inserts for fun. I made it clear: Hands off for three years minimum! … anyone touches him and he gets injured by a vaccine … I'll kill everyone involved down to the pharmaceutical rep!

I thought I had won. We got his Connecticut religious exemption … she could see the difference between the dull-eyed, sniffling kids in the church's cry room. I could go 10 for 10 picking out who got the shots.

But now it's over.

Her older sister is back with the husband she ran away from … a little five-year sexscapade with the D.C. Jerry Maguire.

Why the change of heart?

He threw her out … tossed her aside like a used Kleenex … He tried. You have to give it to him … she wouldn't take the hints … canceling a golf outing to meet her dad … uninviting her from the Kentucky Derby … she was delusional … she didn't realize she was one of many. And an aging model! … what did she expect from an adulterer?

Ultimately, he moved his brother in … to get her lingering remnants out … she still didn't take the hint. He had to spell it out for her: Bon Voyage.

He bought her a Macbook as a parting gift … which she accepted.

But her actual husband impregnated a one-night stand … a little side sexual sabbatical of his own … just playing by the new rules …

they change … now he's a dad. And she wants to come home to play mommy. A failed coup. A rediverted desertion.

She's inundating Freckley Face's iPhone with text messages … not about New York Housewives … the sheer terror of having her bastard child anywhere near our unvaccinated son … she won't do it … say goodbye to all the family functions she never showed up to.

They're mocking me.

Both of them.

My wife who wouldn't take my last name.

Asking for the divorce didn't go over well!

She was very accustomed to comfort and getting her way… red carpet rolled out since birth.

Chapter 22:

—⚮—

Toppled Cairns and the Rise of Karen

"Do you see all these things,'" he asked. "Truly I tell you, not one stone here will be left on another; every one will be thrown down." – Jesus, Matthew 24:2

The most vile, unattractive women … sour puss souls reflected in their faces … they're lined up in the streets by the thousands … multiple cities … adorned with knitted pink vagina hats … they're protesting Donald Trump's vulgarity. Their president.

They're foaming at the mouth. F bombs by the baker's dozen … there's two types. There's really no in-between … middle-class, overweight housewives … with their blah, almost invisible cucked husbands … and emaciated, angry and/or lesbian trust-fund types. With green, blue or no hair … Alone. Alone as could be … especially when with each other.

They're accusing the president of being a Russian spy … deep under cover for decades … waiving the American flag from atop his capitalist-built empire.

227

They have to be the most gullible or evil assholes on the planet … one or the other … the pear-shaped whacko; the chocolate-donut endomorph … noodle-thin lunatic … Evil or Dupe?

They said he wouldn't win. Then they said he couldn't win … multiple recounts! … they don't understand the Electoral College … there's a lot they don't understand.

On Monday they accuse him of being a spy! … they caught him red-handed on the telephone … a big Aha! They got him now!

On Tuesday the president announced his campaign was being spied on.

… the same CNN anchors referencing the recorded telephone conversations on Monday say it's an outlandish, nearly cartoonish accusation on Tuesday.

The pink pussy hats believe both … that he was secretly recorded talking to Russians and that it's ridiculous to think he was recorded talking to Russians. This is their new language.

Anyone with a brain understood, of course Trump was being spied on and, unbelievably, he has to be the dullest billionaire on the plant.

Not one mob deal?

Buy a pizza in New York City?

… money laundering for the Gambino crime family!

He even had his extramarital affairs publicly … no guess work needed … see me today with this gorgeous blonde … tomorrow another.

Unblackmailable when you sin publicly.

Now our first lady is an Eastern European super model.

We've had worse.

Have you seen Barbara Bush?

… the cock on Michael Obama?

You could've asked Joan Rivers … she let it slip … keeping the mouth shut … always the problem.

Justice Scalia … the pillow stuffed in his face at the Bohemian Grove's Texas hunting lodge.

Things slip past these days.

Everything's moving so fast.

Anthony Weiner. Huma Abedin. Jeffrey Epstein … everyone's uncloaking … Harvey Weinstein. Kevin Spacey … pedophile Satanists everywhere! … they're thanking Satan at the Golden Globes … London Fashion Week's Satanic Collection at St. Andrew Holborn's church … high-end sacrificial garb, ceremonial attire for Rihanna.

The church was rebuilt after it was burned to the ground in 1666 … these Satanists have been at it a long time.

They're holding public ceremonies … a little Hocus Pocus to curse Trump.

They're mad he got two extra scoops of ice cream at his own party.

———∿∿∿———

I needed to retreat to the mountains. To save my finances and soul … I was borderline suicidal … you start to project a movie of your future … front row seat … Siskel and Eberts four thumbs down. Very low rating on Rotten Tomatoes.

Young. Committed with so much promise high with God on the shores of Manasquan … another lifetime. Another person.

There were no published books … I don't even write anymore.

All I do is worry about keeping my job. How I can eek out sales from a market that doesn't want to do business with us … only when they need us. Only when they can't get it from China quick enough. Everyone looking out for themselves.

There are no more fights. I'm too old for fighting. Too fragile and too much to lose if injured but not really.

No surfing.

There are no waves in this land.

I've grown tired of driving hours to be disappointed by unorganized, unlined up, small, closed out slop. It is slop.

Trout Town USA … they weren't lying. There are trout here.

No women!

Well, a couple meth heads. Between all of them they have a full set of teeth.

Doesn't keep me from looking as I drive up Main St. … a single block … a small grocery, barber, Chinese fast food … a hipster couple from Brooklyn have opened a wine shop on one side and a wine bar on the other. They're new in town but the wife already heads the Chamber of Commerce … They're motivated. Driven … the rest of us are not.

There're reasons why one would move so far away from everyone.

You're reading mine.

… size 14 parachute.

… I tied it myself.

… no more following the recipe.

Medium Dun wings and split tail with brown dubbed body; orange parachute post.

… drifting.

… drifting across and down the river.

My arm and 9-foot rod fully extended … following at a 45 degree angle … keeping line off the water, removing slack … trying to stay connected … trying to stay connected.

Oh God am I trying to stay connected.

The nearest jui jitsu is 50 miles away so I drive it every night. It's much more reliable than the surf. It's always there.

But most of the time I'm stuck in-between.

Between here and there with a truck full of tile samples.

I'm committed to life.

I'm committed to this drudgery.

It's all for my son now.

It's no longer about me.

I failed.

I know I failed.

I missed a mark that only I could aim for.

I blissfully watched the arrow sail, content … drifting … me and the arrow.

Even now, there's the fool in me expecting the broadhead to sink bullseye.

Americans have unmasked. In the midst of ever present lies … Irrevocable Truth.

Satanists are suing … abortion laws infringe upon their religious freedom. Their most sacred sacrament. As many as they can get.

Not in New York and Virginia. There they can dismember and parcel out a born baby's organs one by one … now you're alive … say good-bye to mommy … now you're cosmetic product; flavoring.

Andrew Cuomo signed the Reproductive Health Act … a smile from ear to ear.

The Democrats aren't fooling around anymore. They're starting to tell the truth.

We want your guns!

Can't be more clear than that.

They're communist now, too. They want your everything.

And they're pissed … for getting caught spying on Trump. For not being able to shame the other half of the country into voting for Hillary Clinton.

Doesn't matter nobody likes her … they don't even like her. But they told us to and we didn't listen. A polite: No Thank You.

They're reviled by themselves.

No one's car, food, diet, paper napkin … nothing is pure enough for these, the most tainted souls.

———— ✸ ————

At first, I didn't understand what all the hubbub was about. They try to scare the hell out of us all the time. It's one of their joys … H1N1. Bird Flu. SARS … blood pouring out of people's eyes; their organs melting from the inside with Ebola … made AIDS looks like child's play.

But it was when I was three days into a Puerto Rican surf trip, a little Home Sweet home … that I knew I … We … *We The People* … we're fucked. Toast.

This Dr. Fauci … who died and made him boss?

Just like that: Beach Closed!

Armed guards at Wilderness.

… Hotel nearly closed.

… have to eat in your room. No going out. No pool for you!

This fucking guy. This villain.

Best friends with Gates and Epstein.

Guess who owns the patented Sign of the Beast?

Don't worry. It's not a microchip … it's "SmartInk" … a million mini-microchips tattooed for you!

Losing your job over the wrong pronoun?

… kid's stuff!

You're going to be singing Lucifer.

Tattooed and locked in your home if you want to eat.

Stuck on Karens shaming the odd nutjob who won't wear his mask over the tomato isle?

… they're just keeping us on ice.

Nobody will listen to me.

0.003 death rate!

That's a lot of zeros.

Nobody has a job.

Everyone's rioting in the streets.

Everyday it's Dr. Fauci says Do This. Dr. Fauci says Do This … Do This!

They're still gambling like drunken sailors on the stock market. They'll keep spinning that wheel right up until they kill us all. Too many ways to do it.

What do you think all those robots are far? AI?

They're for Not For You.

You're as essential as the sixteen-year-old checkout girl … dutifully wearing her mask.

So much exposed in this day of masks.

I'm just glad I have three guns and a stack of ammo under my bed.

<div align="center">~~~</div>

We're finally allowed out of our house but there's nowhere to go.

Well, select corporations.

Wallmart.

Target.

Jeff Bezos is making a fortune.

The perfect business model: Stay in your home.

Don't even try to go to mass.

They'll burn you at the stake!

But JetBlue is packing them into their little guided missile tubes like sardines. Mask: optional.

Get caught flat footed on the ground without that mask?

… some states are calling for the death penalty.

… accessory to murder!

Of course, in San Francisco you can intentionally infect someone with HIV … no parking ticket. Nothing to report … a walk in the park over hypodermic needles.

More customers for Gilead Sciences.

This Covid is some racket.

$30,000 for each hospitalized death.

They're sticking tubes down their throat … choke on that over a 0.003 death rate.

Mandatory tests guaranteed to produce a positive or your money back … avocados, peaches, coconuts, chickens … everything and everyone has Covid yet it's nowhere to be seen. Only Anti-Trumpers … unique vision … all their friends' fiends are dropping like flies.

There's an antidote but it interferes with the control and profits.

Why send a long-proven, inexpensive antimalarial drug to do a Mark of the Beast pandemic job?

Car accidents. Fried to a crisp from chemotherapy … Covid! … I told you. It's everywhere.

It's our new blanket.

CHAPTER 23

JIU-JITSU IN THE DARK

"There's more philosophy on Jiu-Jitsu mats than in any Ivy League school in America." – Master Renzo Gracie

We're fugitives.

We've brown-papered the nearly floor-to-ceiling windows.

… strictly a park-in-the-back; sneak in the backdoor affair.

No lights. No fans.

Not a peep!

These Karens materialize out-of-sight.

Questions galore!

Where's your mask? How much plastic is on the premises?

… we're not supposed to be doing this.

… we're not supposed to be out.

I could murder Dr. Fauci with Bill Gates.

… manhandle that effeminate man in such a way as to entangle him with Fauci, bring them both down and smash the life out of their skulls.

Yet these men control us all.

These Karens don't know they're one snap away from winding up my forever guest in the basement.

I don't answer the phone anymore … forget SPAM or Unknown Caller … any number … particularly local … Board of Health! … they want to know, confirm where you've been … they already know … that's why they're calling.

Quarantines for entering and exiting New York State.

… have they seen the traffic at the George Washington Bridge?

Any given day I'm squirming back and forth across borders … Connecticut, New York, New Jersey and Massachusetts.

My family has uninvited me and my boy for life.

… for living.

… for jui-jitsu.

… for outlawness.

I wouldn't want to be their Jewish neighbor in Nazi Germany.

100% collaborators

Definitely the Do-As-Your-Told type.

For the love of your neighbor.

A little push.

A little helping hand onto the train.

I'm not going to tell them it's hysterical, a real hoot … listening to their upcoming plans.

Thought Covid was a surprise inconvenience?

Childs play!

They're lined up outside the shower.

They used to think I was crazy ... now they want to know ... Coming Attractions ... now they're curious.

Unlike Noah, I've learned to keep my mouth shut.

Enjoy the surprise.